"The concept of persons—especially leaders—thriving, has been addressed from psychological, sociological, philosophical, and functional perspectives but rarely in an integrative and wholistic way as Ellen has done. This is a must-read that provides a theological basis for equipping and enabling human thriving. Ellen is uniquely experienced and equipped to shape such a model and explain its foundation, having facilitated the process of human thriving in regional, national, and global settings. Over the span of over 50 years of research study and teaching and learning facilitation I have not found an equal to the value this resource adds."

        — Paul E. Magnus, PhD.
           President Emeritus, Chair of Leadership & Management Emeritus, Briercrest College & Seminary

A THEOLOGY OF THRIVING

ELLEN DUFFIELD

For contact and ordering information, visit: www.ellenduffield.com

Quantity sales: Special discounts may be available on quantity purchases by corporations, educational institutions, and others. For details, contact the author.

Orders by trade bookstores and wholesalers. Please contact Ingram:
North America - Tel: (800) 937-0152
All other areas - Tel: (615) 213-5000
or visit www.ingramcontent.com

Printed in the United States of America

Publisher's Cataloging-in-Publication data
Duffield, Ellen.
   A theology of thriving: belonging, being, and contributing / by Ellen Duffield.
   118p. 15.24 x 22.86 cm.
   ISBN 978-1-9992606-3-7
   1. Religion. 2. Christian Theology. 3. General. I. Duffield, Ellen.

First Edition
23 22 21 20 19 18 / 10 9 8 7 6 5 4 3 2 1

Cover and Interior Design: Shadow River Ink

26 Then God said, "Let us make man[a] in our image, after our likeness. And let them have dominion over the fish of the sea and over the birds of the heavens and over the livestock and over all the earth and over every creeping thing that creeps on the earth."

27 So God created man in his own image,
    in the image of God he created him;
    male and female he created them.

28 And God blessed them. And God said to them, "Be fruitful and multiply and fill the earth and subdue it, and have dominion over the fish of the sea and over the birds of the heavens and over every living thing that moves on the earth."

Genesis 1:26-28 ESV

Contents

Introduction
— Living as God's Beloved

IT WAS THE DARKEST, MOST PAINFUL SEASON OF MY LIFE TO DATE. I would tell you about it, except it is not my story, and people I love dearly, who have been hurt enough already, might be hurt more in the telling. In the long months of disillusionment and grieving, I turned to the ancient language of lament. "Why, Lord? Why O Why? Why did You create people, so we are prone to do things like this?" Days that turned to weeks that turned to months of silence. Silence.

Then one day, a quiet Voice answered, "I didn't." And that Voice, piercing my heart with its grieving and understanding, changed everything.

The gift wrapped in the tatters of this excruciating season was the same gift offered in every loss — renewed intimacy with a God who cares and insight into the things that sit heavy on God's heart.

This is not my story. This is that story. It is the story of *the Beloved*.

More than thirty different names reference God in the book of Isaiah alone. Some are more commonly used and anticipated — Creator, Judge, King. Some take a bit more getting used to — Saviour, Potter, Shepherd. And one stands out as too intimate for us to even imagine — Beloved. "Let me sing for my beloved my love song."[1]

Traditionally this name has only been used by contemplatives, mystics, and poets who dared to describe a relationship with God in such personal terms. Yet, amazingly, the invitation is extended to all.

---

1. Isaiah 5:1a ESV

To call God our Beloved seems audacious. To believe God calls *us* the Beloved seems almost impossible. Yet it is true. Scattered throughout scripture, with increasing intensity and significance, God invites us to this realization.

This kind of relationship offers the promise of many blessings, not least of which is found in Isaiah, where God says, "you are precious in my eyes and honoured, and I love you."[2]

They include:
    God's redemption of us. Isaiah 43:1
    God's presence and protection around us. Isaiah 43:2,5
    God's revelation to us. Isaiah 43: 10-13
    God's forgiveness for us. Isaiah 43:25
    God's Spirit within us. Isaiah 44:3
    God's peace upon us. Isaiah 48:17,18

With these gifts comes a calling:
    To glorify God with our lives and worship. Isaiah 43:7
    To be witnesses to the world of God's goodness. Isaiah 43:10, 12
    To be open to the new ways that God opens in the wilderness. Isaiah 43:18-19

These gifts are described in the language of family. "See what kind of love the Father has given to us, that we should be called children of God . . . Beloved, we are God's children."[3]

In the Bible and in our world, this image of beauty and love is juxtaposed against brokenness and hatred.

---

2.   Isaiah 43:4 ESV
3.   1 John 3:1,2a ESV

Perhaps you are grieving the brokenness you see in yourself and others? Feeling alone, misunderstood, or perhaps worst of all, invisible? Perhaps you are wondering if this is all there is?

Have you bruised your chest, beating it and asking, "Why?" Or worse, buried those questions under layers of complacency, skepticism or busyness? You are not alone.

We live in a beautiful yet broken world. But this is not the way it was meant to be. And more importantly, this is not the way it has to be.

1

*God's Ideal for Humanity from the Beginning
— In the Language and Lessons of Creation*

SEEKING TO UNDERSTAND what God intended for humanity, I began in Genesis 1, planning to read through the whole Bible in search of insight. Of course, I am not alone in this quest. Psalm 8:4 records the question: "What [are human beings] that you are mindful of them?" Questions of identity, purpose and connection to the Divine have saturated our thinking since time began. Who am I? Does God really exist, and if so, what is God like? What does God think of me? Why am I here? And, for many of us: how can I contribute in God-honouring ways when I am wracked with insecurity, brokenness, and selfishness . . . and live in a world filled with conflict, distraction and disillusionment?

All these years later, I am unable to move past the opening of Genesis. In these chapters, we find hints of what we were created for, tantalizing insights into what it means to thrive. In them, we see a picture of the completeness, wholeness, harmony and reciprocity that in Old Testament language is called *Shalom*. Jesus calls it *Abundant Life,* and He demonstrates the countless ways that God longs for us to experience it. Not prosperity, mind you, nor lack of suffering, but a fullness of life that celebrates beauty and gives brokenness meaning.

In Genesis 1, we read of God speaking the universe into being. Each of the creative accounts begins with the same language and follows a similar pattern. God says, "'Let there be' . . . and it was so . . . and God saw that it was good." This pattern repeats five times.

The first snapshot of the Creator reveals the Spirit of God hovering over the expanse like a stingray skimming the surface of the deeps or an eagle soaring on rising currents — protective, commanding, and standing ready over her young.

Out of the swirling waters, order begins to emerge. Light brings contrast to darkness. Waters are gathered as if by Divine hands. Stars are flung against the backdrop of space, and the sun's intensity burns away the morning mist. Volcanoes erupt, and tectonic plates shift as above-ground creatures are spoken into being — bees and birds of prey, octopuses and orangutans, clams with hundreds of piercing eyes and codfish swarming in schools of thousands. Fireflies land on exotic flowers as owls blink in the sun and sloths amble up trees to taste the new-formed leaves.

This universe is so resplendent that the angels don't just sing about heaven. They sing about the earth, crying, "Holy, holy, holy is the Lord of hosts; the whole earth is full of his glory."[4] Christie Purifoy reflects on this, saying, "the earth is full of His glory. It soaks everything, seeps from every seam . . . we droop beneath the heavy weight of glory in the humid air and spy its mystery in the spider that scuttles away."[5]

Then suddenly, language and pattern change. God says, "Let us make *adam* [humanity] in our image, after our likeness. And let *them* have dominion over the fish of the sea and over the birds of the heavens and over the livestock and over all the earth and over every creeping thing that creeps on the earth."[6]

Conversation. Community. Let *us* make. Let *them* have.

---

4.   Isaiah 6:3
5.   Christie Purifoy, *Roots and Wings*, 201.
6.   Genesis 1:26 (emphasis added)

Have what? At least three things, as we will see.

In the first poetry of the Bible, the narrator repeats:

"So God created *adam* in his own image,

in the image of God he created him;

male and female he created them."[7]

Oneness and diversity. Human and Divine. Male and female. Individual and community.

Desmond Tutu once said: "Differences are not intended to separate, to alienate. We are different precisely in order to realize our need of one another."

Returning to prose, the narrator continues: "And God blessed them. And God said to them, 'be fruitful and multiply and fill the earth and subdue it and have dominion over it...and it was so. And God saw everything that He had made, and it was very good.'"[8]

What is it that was good? What were we created for?

Three stunning gifts:

1. The offer of God-sized intimacy. "Let us . . . make them." We are created out of the community that is God and set into a human and environmental community, infused and embraced by our relationship to God. We are created to Belong.

2. The gift of God-stamped identity. "In our image and after our likeness." We are created to *Be* our true selves — each unique yet linked in shared humanity and God createdness.

3. The invitation to partner with God in stewardship. We are created to *Contribute* — to care for what is and co-create what could be.

_____

7. Genesis 1:27
8. Genesis 1:28

There may be countless ways of describing and visualizing this passage. I draw it as a simple triangle with three separate yet deeply connected and overlapping parts.

Belonging

THE CREATION OF HUMANITY BEGINS with "Then God said, 'Let us.'" If we are not careful, we might jump over this first recorded conversation without recognizing how profound it is. In each of the creation accounts, the Triune God speaks complex systems and countless creatures into being, but here, in the creation of humanity, we see God deliberately framing those words as conversation. Scholars wonder at who is included in this conversation. Father, Son, and Spirit — a theological concept not yet developed in scripture? God and the universe — an intriguing idea? God and the angels — equally intriguing? Something else? The answer to that question is beyond my theological understanding. Yet the context beckons me towards a God who is One and more than One. A God who values relationship.

Try to imagine this scene. Father, Son and Spirit interact in what the ancient church — unable to find language to describe the uniqueness and interconnectedness of the Three Persons of the Godhead — called the Circle Dance of Love. Joy and creativity abound in this Dance. Beauty and diversity unfold in the Dance's wake. Imagine what it must have been like as God dreams and plans. Motivated by love, God envisions what is possible, adding water that swirls, flowers that unfurl, and ferns that spiral for the sheer delight of it.

Then God pauses, as if to catch the Creative Breath and says, "let us . . . make them." We are birthed from community into community. "Let us . . . make them." We are created to Belong.

From the intimacy of the Godhead Adam and Eve emerge.

From intimate acts of men and women every child thereafter will be born.

Within the richness of Creator and creation, we live and move and have our being.

As South African Archbishop Desmond Tutu explains, "the first law of our being is that we are set in a delicate network of interdependence with our fellow human beings and with the rest of God's creation." When we are denied these connections or choose to ignore them, we become bereft, profoundly undermining our ability to thrive.

God knew that it was not good for man to be alone. So a helpmate is provided, a strong helper or protector (*ezer*), to partner with him in work and journey with him in life. While we could restrict this to our desire for a significant other, it clearly extends beyond this to our need for family, for friends, and for healthy teams and organizations and communities.

Remarkably, God walks with these newly made creatures in the cool of the garden. Relationship with God and others is freely given, not only as a generous gift but also as an integral part of what it means to be human — to be human in relationship to the Divine. When we think about engaging with others, we usually think about other people. However, in the creation account, the first relationship is with God. This is true at an individual level and at a corporate level. Later, as the Hebrew people left Mount Sinai on their way to the Promised Land, Moses begs God, saying "if your presence will not go up with *me*, do not bring *us* up from here . . . Is it not in your going with us so that we are distinct, I and your people, from every other people on the face of the earth?"[1] And later yet, Jesus came as "Immanuel, which means, God with us." The New Testament invites our involvement both as a personal follower of Jesus and also as part of the communal family of God.

This relationship with others is modeled in the picture of unity, sacrificial love and shared responsibility that we see in the Godhead.

In Western thinking it is less common to reflect on what it means to be in healthy relationship with ourselves, or with the rest of creation. You might want to pause to think about those for a moment.

---

1. Exodus 33:14-16

The community God creates is multifaceted and multi-layered. It includes deep and authentic relationships with Him, with other people, with ourselves, and with the rest of creation. We could draw this in a simple diagram that looks like this.

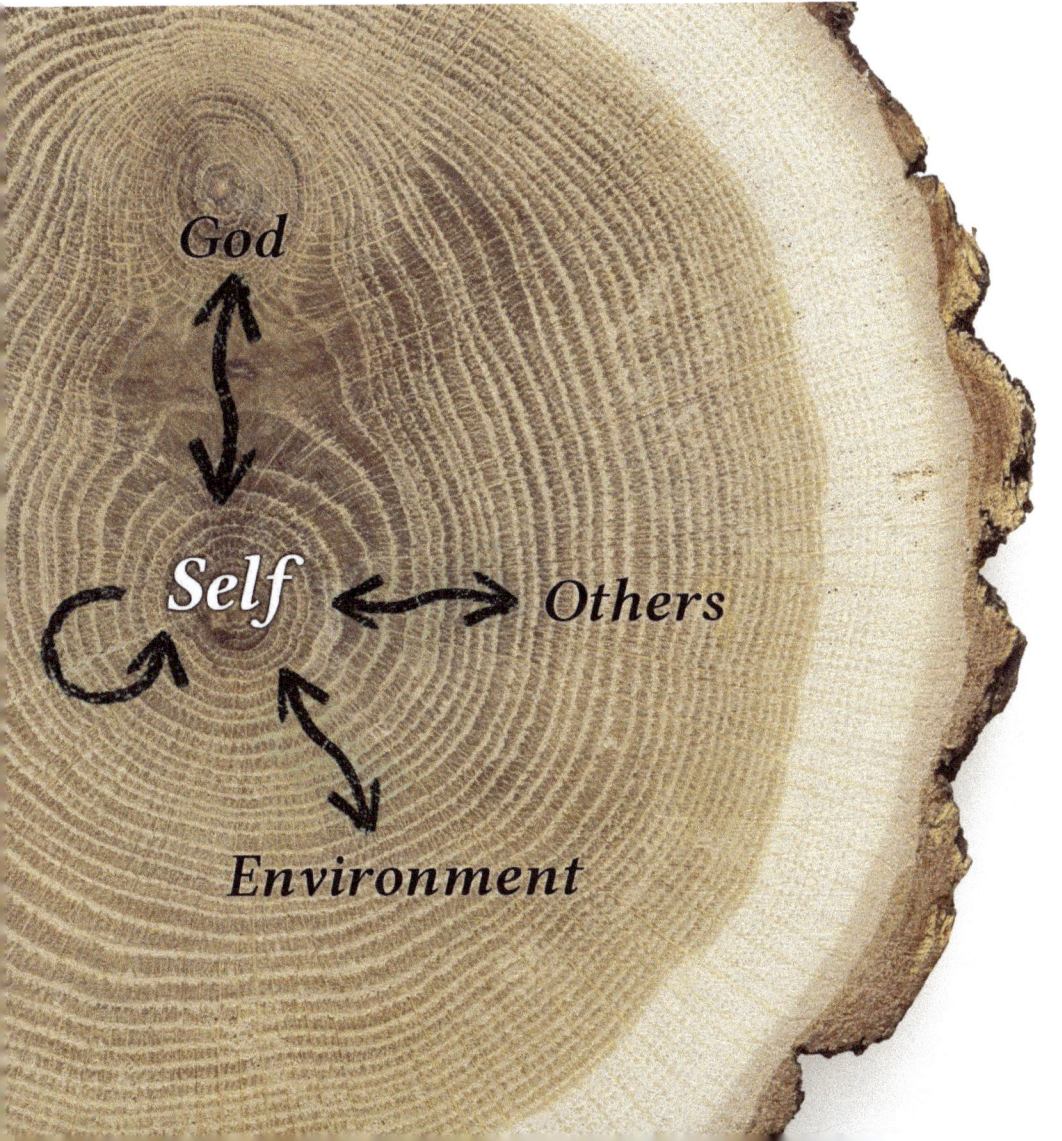

These profoundly modern concepts stood in sharp contrast to the teachings of dominant cultures at the time that Genesis was written. In the Canaanite worldview humanity was created as a result of a power struggle between warring gods, not an act of love within God. The prevailing view of women was so low they would never be presented as a strong partner. The Canaanites believed humans' role was to do the menial tasks the gods did not want to bother with, not collaborate with God to steward the earth. In contrast, Genesis 1 shows God discussing, and then lovingly creating every part of the universe. God invites Adam, and later Eve, to converse in the Garden, and work in and keep it, continuing the work of naming the creatures. While it may be difficult to understand the importance of these distinctives in our day, they were revolutionary!

I have been trying to imagine God's delight as humanity was first envisioned. Fjords and fossils now matched by the richness of cultures and music, sunsets festooned with feasting, childrens' lullabies and adults' lovemaking. Who suggested laughter I wonder? And how were the synapses of our brains and the cells of our bodies planned? One thing I am sure of, each part was lovingly discussed, for it was love that necessitated creation and love that spoke every part of us into being.

We may know how it feels to step barefooted onto dew-wet grass in the early morning, to look with awe at snow-capped mountains from the window of a plane or to hold one's snorkelled breath as spiny fish swim between our nose and the reef below. Yet can we begin to imagine how it must have felt for Adam and Eve to step into the world God created? Did they shout for joy at each discovery or tiptoe like children in a world of untold wonders?

Less yet can we pretend to know what it must have been like for God, watching the universe unfold. Angels and creation sharing in the delight. How very good it was. A beautiful garden. A measureless universe, and God walking with Adam and Eve in the cool of the evening.

We are birthed out of community into community, entering both nature's circle of life and God's circle of love. We are created to belong. No wonder this is our deepest longing and our greatest fear.

This is also a lens through which to look at life and ministry. Bonhoeffer reflected deeply on this. He "sought to place God's presence somewhere other than in the subjective and individualistic experience. Instead he placed God's presence in the social experience of community, in relationships . . . relationships being the place where we meet the presence of God, the place where God embraces us."[2] In fact, "the tissue that holds church and world together, maintaining their connection, is the reality of relationship."[3]

We meet God who *dwells in relationship*, in relationships. We meet ourselves through relationships. We meet the world through relationships, in which God works in both the beauty and the brokenness, and draws creation toward its ultimate restoration.

The world meets Christ in the community of the church, for this is where "Christ is concretely present in the world... not as an invisible entity . . . [but] in the relationships that hold the community together as they love one another through the sharing of the sacraments and submission to the Word of God."[4] In fact, Christ is so present in the world that whatever we do for the least of these we do for Christ, and whatever we do not do for the least we do not do for Him.

Belonging could not be more integral to who God is, who we are, and how we engage with Divinity and humanity. Belonging spaces, properly understood, are of course much more than mere social spaces or friend groups. True spaces of belonging are sacred spaces, where God lives and moves — redeeming, reconciling, and recreating. They are safe yet brave spaces where the love of Christ is present because Christ is present. Perhaps this is why relationships that are *used* for

---

2. Andrew Root, *Revisiting Relational Ministry,* 105-6.
3. Andrew Root, *Revisiting Relational Ministry,* 106.
4. Andrew Root, *Revisiting Relational Ministry,* 106-8.

ministry (vs. relationships that develop genuinely and organically) are just as dangerous as relationships that are *misused* in ministry.

Many years ago, I took our firstborn child out shopping. After a day of staring at kneecaps from his stroller, I could tell that the poor boy was weary. Putting him into his car seat I heard him forlornly whisper a word I had not heard him say before. It was the word "home." All these years later I feel the tug on my heart that word elicited. Unable to speak a full sentence he craved what all of us do — home. Children are born wanting this. We spend our lives searching for this. God designed us to need this. We are created to belong.

We would do almost anything to find our place, but we also spurn the vulnerability of true community. We crave, yet fear, to be seen. We desire, yet dread commitment. We settle for false communities where belonging is replaced with shallow substitutes and conditional love. We selfishly pursue places where we feel safe even if others are unwelcome.

Regardless of our vocation, once we join the Circle Dance this pursuit changes. Creating spaces where our selves and others can truly thrive becomes our primary calling. And, following in God's footsteps, dialogue becomes one of our greatest building blocks.

While we rightly hesitate to picture God, the ancient art of iconography gives us one way to imagine the Trinity in conversation.

In The Trinity, *Andrei Rublev's icon of Abraham's visit by the three angels, we see the Godhead represented in deep dialogue. Seated around a table rich with symbols of the Eucharist there is room for a guest. We are that invited guest and there is always, miraculously, room for one more. As millions upon millions come home to the table they find that there is always room for one more.*

Andrei Rublev. The Trinity, *or* The Hospitality of Abraham. *1411 or 1425 - 27. On display at the Tretyakov Gallery, Moscow. Public domain image.*

Art and literature are riddled with this longing. L. M. Montgomery's astonishingly popular heroine in *Anne of Green Gables* is an orphan who, deprived of a home and a "bosom friend," creates imaginary friends and grandiose stories of a former life. Her world is transformed when she is finally adopted by an elderly and flawed couple named the Cuthberts. Anne no longer needs to make up stories of family, friends, or home. Her real name becomes enough. Perhaps this is why so many love Anne and travel the world to see her literary birthplace. She speaks to the orphan in each of us, longing to find our true home.

At the other end of the literature spectrum, Mary Shelley's classic, *Frankenstein*, explores deeply political, philosophical, and personal themes. Mary sees in a waking dream and then writes in horrific detail of a monster who becomes a monster only when it realizes that it will never fit in anywhere.

Beauty and the Beast, Pip in Dicken's *Great Expectations*, the Hobbits in Tolkien's *Lord of the Rings*, Jane Austen's *Emma*, Shakespeare's *Hamlet*, the characters of almost every novel, sitcom, and movie tell the same story of looking for a place to belong.

In an interesting but horrifying case study, anthropologist Colin Turnball wrote about a semi-nomadic tribal people, the Ik, whose traditional grounds were severely restricted by the Ugandan government. Their society collapsed. Children were shunned, family units disintegrated, people foraged alone and stole food from each other. Turnball concluded that, "if we remove our sense of belonging to each other, no matter what our material and social conditions are, survival, acquisition, and selfish triumphalism will endure at the cost of humanity."[5] Sadly, we see this replicated in colonized communities and displaced peoples around the world.

---

5. Colin Turnbull, *The Mountain People*, quoted in Adrienne Clarkson, *Belonging*, 5-7.

Humanity depends on relationship. It is rooted in our creation and reinforced by our culture. As Canadian Adrienne Clarkson writes, "It is society that makes it possible for us to develop ourselves as human beings . . . we are all born biologically from a union. And it is as part of a group that we learn to belong."[6]

While in the West we may read the language of belonging through an individual lens it is important to remember that most of the Bible is written to the collective. Together *we* are God's Beloved, *we* are invited to Belong, *we* are the People of God.

This in no way detracts from the possibility of a personal relationship with God within this greater community. Just the opposite. It is precisely because we are God's family that we may each approach as a Beloved child.[7] God longs for this kind of relationship with us. Notice however that when Paul prays for God's very best for us he prays, "that Christ may dwell in your hearts through faith — that you being rooted and grounded in love, may have strength to comprehend with all the saints what is the breadth and length and height and depth, and to know the love of Christ that surpasses knowledge, that you may be filled with all the fullness of God."[8] In a powerful twist, the mark of grounding in God's love is that we love one another. "Beloved, if God so loved us, we also ought to love one another. No one has ever seen God; if we love one another, God abides in us and his love is perfected in us."[9]

The kind of relationship envisioned in Genesis, and repeated through scripture, is one of profound intimacy. In Isaiah 43:1-10, we hear God cry out, "thus says the LORD, he who created you, O Jacob, he who formed you, O Israel; 'Fear not for I have redeemed you; I have called you by name, you are mine. When you pass through the

---

6. Adrienne Clarkson, *Belonging*, 1-4.
7. 1 John 3:2
8. Ephesians 3:17-19
9. 1 John 4:11,12

waters, I will be with you . . . You are my witnesses, declares the LORD, and my servant whom I have chosen, that you may know and believe me.'" God uses the language of marriage as a metaphor for this intimacy.[10] We are Beloved, formed, and called by God.

Such love is not easy to offer or receive. Brené Brown writes that "we cultivate love when we allow our most vulnerable and powerful selves to be deeply seen and known and when we honor the spiritual connection that grows from that offering with trust, respect, kindness and affection. Love is not something we give or get, it is something that we nurture and grow, a connection that can only be cultivated between two people when it exists within each one of them. We can only love others as much as we love ourselves. Shame, blame, disrespect, betrayal and the withholding of affection damage the roots from which love grows. Love can only survive these injuries if they are acknowledged, healed and rare."[11]

What would it look like to feel at home in your neighbourhood? Your school? Your place of work?

Willie James Jennings' book *After Whiteness: An Education in Belonging* provocatively claims that "the cultivation of belonging should be the goal of all education — not just any type of belonging, but a profoundly creaturely belonging that performs the returning of the creature to the Creator."[12] He takes it further saying, "theological education is supposed to open up sites where we enter the struggle to rethink our people. We think them again, but now with others who must rethink their people. And in this thinking together we begin to see what we have not seen before: we belong to each other."[13]

When my husband and I visited New Zealand, a friend arranged for us to hike with a Māori guide. He picked us up in his car, and

---

10.   See, for example Matthew 9:14-15; Ephesians 5:25-27; 2 Corinthians 11:2; Revelation 19:7, 21:2.
11.   Brené Brown, *The Gifts of Imperfection*, 26.
12.   Willie James Jennings, *After Whiteness*, 11.
13.   Willie James Jennings, *After Whiteness*, 10.

along the way peppered us with questions about ourselves and our heritage. He also freely shared about himself, his people's history and his extended family. In our worldview, this constituted small talk. Yet nothing could have been further from the truth. This wise, godly, and kind gentleman was opening his world to us, and willingly entering ours. His Māori and Christian mindset taught him the importance of knowing others well. By finding sufficient points of connection, he sought to learn from our differences and commonalities. It turned out that we had ancestors from the same continent, and on hearing this he smiled broadly, saying: "We have discovered how we are family, now we can go, as family, on the hike."

Willie Jennings explains the power of this kind of connection: "The belonging I am envisioning here superintends all other forms of belonging, drawing [us] to healing light and redemptive life."[14] We do not just belong to God, ourselves, and a few close loved ones. We belong to what Jennings calls "the crowd" and it is within the crowd that we see God and become like Him. Reflecting on Mark 5:1 Jennings writes, "People shouting, screaming, crying, pushing, shoving, calling out to Jesus, 'Jesus help me,' 'Jesus over here.' People being forced to press up against each other to get to Jesus . . . people who hate each other, who would prefer not to be next to each other . . . all pressing to hear Jesus . . . caught together under his word . . . The crowd was not his disciples, but it was the condition for discipleship . . . the crowd is necessary to see God's overwhelming compassion."[15] The crowd is the condition for discipleship and the place where we see God's compassion. No wonder we avoid crowds.

Fear may tempt us to settle for conditional, shallow acceptance. Fitting in seems sufficient when true belonging feels elusive. Shallow relationships may be better than none at all, and safer than those

_____

14. Willie James Jennings, *After Whiteness*, 12.
15. Willie James Jennings, *After Whiteness*, 12-13.

that insist on going deeper. Hiding our true selves behind masks, sarcasm, or indifference are common self-protective practices, but beneath it, we are crying out to be seen, to be known, and to be loved.

In his book *The Meaning of Marriage* Timothy Keller explains this beautifully, writing that "to be loved but not known is comforting but superficial. To be known and not loved is our greatest fear. But to be fully known and truly loved is, well, a lot like being loved by God. It is what we need more than anything. It liberates us from pretence, humbles us, and strengthens us for any difficulty life can throw at us."

Genesis begins with a picture of interconnectedness, a social and spiritual ecosystem that is mirrored throughout the universe. This interconnectedness has wide-ranging consequences for creation and for us human creatures. Mother Teresa once said that "if we have no peace, it is because we have forgotten that we belong to each other." Could it really be that simple and profound?

This connection also comes with responsibility. In 1977, testifying before the Royal Commission on the Northern Environment, Grand Chief John Kelly described how the Ojibway were cheated by Treaty 3. He pointed out that people work together by enlarging their circle, not by hierarchy, sheer will, or force of power. "As the years go by, the circle of the Ojibway gets bigger and bigger. Canadians of all colours and religions are entering the circle. You might feel that you have roots somewhere else, but in reality, you are right here with us. I do not know if you feel the throbbing of the land in your chest as I do . . . but you can no longer escape my fate as the soil turns barren and rivers poison. Much against my will and probably yours, time and circumstance have put us together in the same circle. And so I do not come to plead with you to save me from the monstrous stranger of capitalist greed and technology. I come to inform you that my danger is your danger too. My genocide is your genocide."[16]

----

16. John Kelly, quoted in Adrienne Clarkson, *Belonging*, 5-7.

This circle can be applied at team, organizational, community, and national levels. Ultimately, however, to understand our belonging is to see ourselves within the greater body of all humanity as well as our particular heritage — whether that heritage is by birth or as one chosen through adoption or fostering.

The symbol of a circle is powerful and inclusive. It shuns hierarchy and privilege. It encourages collaboration. As Adrienne Clarkson adds, "a circle allows everyone to see each other, touch each other, and lose fear of each other . . . In a circle, we no longer ask 'Who is my neighbour?' because our neighbour is right beside us . . . and we cannot deny to others the right to belong. It is the most profound acknowledging of our belonging to the human race . . . we take our place and let others do the same."[17]

Perhaps this is why early Christian mothers and fathers pictured the Godhead as a Circle Dance. Perhaps that is why many cultures have participated in circle dances throughout history.

However, it is not the shape but the shoulder-to-shoulder-ness of it that matters. Many years ago, I had the privilege of spending a week at a spiritual retreat in Iona, Scotland. The experience was powerful on many levels, but one story will suffice here. In the kindness of God my visit overlapped with the presence of forty-eight German theologians, a handful of individuals who had come alone (or with one other as I had) and twenty-four guests from *L'Arche* — a community of caregivers and people with severe disabilities who live together as friends. When it came time for communion I entered the beautiful sanctuary, expecting to sit scattered amongst the pews as we had each day thus far that week. To my surprise, the pews were all blocked off and long benches had been brought from the dining hall to line the central aisle. In order to fit all of us, we had to sit very closely together, squeezing ever closer as each new person came. It took a long time

---

17. Adrienne Clarkson, *Belonging*, 5-7.

to get everyone into position as people were moved from wheelchairs onto the benches, supported by those around them. The aisle was so narrow that our knees almost touched those sitting opposite. It was awkwardly and intentionally intimate. The first reader stood and read "For we are one Body . . . " Never had I experienced this truth so powerfully. Thousands of miles from home and amidst strangers, I had been squeezed into the family, and together we gathered at our Father's table. I belonged to these people and they belonged to me because we all belonged to the Beloved. Simple. Sacred. Life-changing. That's what Belonging is.

One research organization asked thousands of people questions about diversity and inclusion. They concluded, that "diversity takes you from zero to one, while *inclusion* takes you from one to ten."[18] Inclusion is so much more than just diversity. One factor stood out across all demographics — a sense of belonging. "I feel like I *belong* at my company," was the statement that most correlated to workplace engagement in every subgroup.[19] The correlation was even more significant for those who are underrepresented numerically.[20] This is critical.

People who feel that they belong become more willing to challenge themselves and are more resilient.[21] While belonging may seem like a nebulous characteristic it can be both measured and developed. Subtle and even unconscious cues can also quickly undermine it.

Being excluded or wounded at work is painful, being excluded or wounded by caregivers early in life is devastating. Refused connection to others at this critical point, we can become disconnected from ourselves. The journey home takes time and grace and intentionality.

---

18. Hyon S. Chu, "New Technology Industry Diversity and Inclusion Report, 2017," *Culture Amp.* Emphasis added.
19. Ibid.
20. Ibid.
21. *6 Ways to Foster Belonging in the Workplace: Taking Diversity & Inclusion to the Next Level,* a Culture Amp eBook, 6.

In one concerning study, Ikea surveyed twenty-two thousand people in twenty-two countries and found that only 57% of people who lived alone or with family felt a sense of belonging in their own home. That number was even lower for those living with friends or strangers, at only 34%.[22]

We are a disconnected people who were created to Belong — and to create spaces where all are welcome. This work is more important and sacred than we might think. And somehow, in deep mystery, God dwells in the midst of it. 1 John 4:12 teaches that "if we love one another, God abides in us, and his love is perfected in us."[23] In an age that celebrates independence this casts a countercultural message of God-dependence and healthy interdependence with others. While not common, we can capture glimpses of it if we keep our eyes open.

As a student, our daughter lived in the basement of a family home. The single mother upstairs had raised her biological children and had also fostered and adopted countless more. Many of these children had experienced a horrific past and carried profound wounds. While driving across Canada, the mom stopped at our home with three of her children. I took the two boys for a walk to show them around the kids' camp where we worked. Unfortunately, they were visiting between sessions so most activities were closed. Seeing some young children participating in one such activity they asked why they were allowed to do so. I tried to explain that "staff kids" had certain privileges. Not missing a beat the one young man explained that as our daughter lived with them and was therefore part of their family that made us all family and I could, therefore, rightly let them participate as a staff kid. While on one level I knew that I was being conned, on another I was touched by the simple way I had been so readily adopted. Something

---

22. Kelsey Campbell-Dollaghan, "A new Ikea report is an unsettling look at life in the 21st century."
23. See also John 15, 17:4; 1 John 3:11,16, 4:16, 5:2.

in the way this boy was being raised by his mom had taught him to open wide his arms to newcomers. In Jesus we have been given the Spirit of Sonship. What a gift to receive and to extend to others!

We belong to God and to each other; imprinted with the very fingerprint of our Creator. For some of us it may be hidden under layers of neglect, regret, or abuse. The unfolding of those layers is itself a sacred calling. It happens in our shared journey to discover whose we are, what it means to love in Jesus name, and to be the communal, Beloved, Bride of God.

Where have you experienced true Belonging?

How vibrant are your key relationships?

The deeper we delve into this concept the more we see how crucial it is to work as "space-makers." Space at the table for the one who has never yet been invited. Space in the conversation for other opinions. Space in our hearts for one more.

Jesus gave everything to make room for the outcast and a way back for the one who had wandered off.

He taught a theology of space-making. Reflecting on this causes me to ponder:

Could hospitality truly be so important in Jesus' New Order?

Where am I creating this kind of space for others?

What does authentic welcome look like in my world?

This is more difficult than it sounds. What creates a sense of belonging for one person can make another feel excluded. Our stories can include or exclude. Our expectations of welcome or intimacy can be unrealistic. Our own woundedness can create the desire to rescue others and be needed, or to shun the vulnerability it requires to live in honest relationships in this messy world. Walter Brueggemann says Leviticus 26:6 and Ezekiel 24:25-29 "show *shalom* in all its power. It is a well-being that exists in the midst of threats...salvation...in the very places where people always have to cope with anxiety, struggle for survival and deal with temptation. It is well-being of a very personal kind... but it is also deliberately corporate. If there is to be well-being, it will not be just for isolated, insulated individuals; it is rather security and prosperity granted to a whole community... Shalom comes only to the inclusive, embracing community that excludes none."[24]

Counter intuitively, our work is not just to be good hosts, our work is also to learn to be good guests — our willingness to go to tables where we feel less comfortable; to be the one who stands out; to make it safe for others to let us into their hearts and homes. As Kat Armas so poignantly notes, "I don't particularly agree with the saying we need to make space at the table for people on the margins. People on the margins have their own tables. . . is it really loving if you force someone to leave their own table – the one they've prepared — so they can sit at yours? . . . Jesus . . . turned table practices on their head . . . perhaps we should too . . . regular guests at unfamiliar tables with only the motives of listening and learning."[25]

What unfamiliar tables have you been frequenting recently?

What are you hearing and learning there?

Living as the Beloved changes us. Every part of us.

And Living as the Beloved enables us to be our true selves, as we will see in the next chapter.

Prayer: "May the God of endurance and encouragement grant you to live in such harmony with one another, in accord with Christ Jesus, that together with one voice you may glorify the God and Father of our Lord Jesus Christ. Therefore welcome one another as Christ has welcomed you, for the glory of God."[26]

---

24. Walter Brueggemann, *Living Towards a Vision,* 16.
25. Kat Armas, *Abuelita Faith,* 137.
26. Romans 15:5-7

» *Where have you experienced true community and belonging? What has it taught about God's Nature?*

» *How has being part of God's family shaped your sense of rootedness?*

» *Do you agree that experiencing "the crowd" is important to our ability to experience and express God's compassion, and the place of discipleship?*

» *How do you respond to Mother Teresa's thought that if we have no peace, it is because we have forgotten that we belong to one another?*

» *This book talks about a theology of space-making. What role does hospitality play in that for you? How are you intentionally creating places of welcome and belonging for others?*

» *Over involvement or identification with others creates its own challenges. List a few.*

» *How does thinking about your relationship with the natural environment as part of belonging influence your thinking?*

» *There are natural tensions between belonging and being. We could describe some of these as community vs. individuality, unity vs. freedom, identification with the group vs. self-differentiation, personal vs. corporate, and attachment vs. independence. Do you find yourself currently navigating one of these tensions?*

Being

IN THE WEST, we have honoured *what we are* (our identity) *over who we are part of* (our community). We have suffered as a result. When I started working on this model, I inadvertently demonstrated my Western bias by placing Being as the foundation of the triangle.

Identity, however, is the *second* thing mentioned in the Genesis passage. Parts of the world with more communal worldviews offer a less individualistic perspective. Belonging precedes and dramatically informs Being. Whatever your worldview, we can agree that, in many ways, we discover who we are in the eyes and responses of others. Our sense of self develops amid, and in response to, our responsive community — or lack thereof. The Genesis 1 Creation account speaks directly to the question, "Who am I?" God says, "Let us make humanity in our image and after our likeness." Again we must pause here lest we skim over something incredibly profound. Who are we? We are creatures spoken into being by God, stamped with Divine authority and sealed with God's identity. Wow. Almost parenthetically, the passage finishes, "So God created humanity in His own image . . . and it was so."

By creating from community and calling us into community, God gives us the opportunity for a relationship with Himself and with others. By creating us in His own image, God gives us the opportunity for a relationship with *ourselves* — with both the One-of-a-kind who is reflected in us and the one-of-a-kind who is us.

And here is the first place of creative tension. To discover ourselves, we must in some way separate from others, even become other. This is our development journey, and it does not end when we are finally old enough to drive or vote. Navigating the relationship of unique identity and communal belonging takes wisdom and maturity. The group does not determine us, and neither are we individuals who develop and act in isolation. We dance in a hall of mirrors, offering countless reflections and distortions of who we are. It restricts or enlarges our blinders. Seeking to make meaning of all this, we must return to the place of true knowing.

We are made in the image of God.

In an era of achievement, comparison, and actualization, Christianity teaches that "personhood is not an accomplishment; it is a gift . . . our true self . . . the self we are becoming in God — is something we receive from God. Any other identity is of our own making and is an illusion. Knowing ourselves must therefore begin by knowing the self that is known to God."[27] Without this sense-maker our quest for self can take so many unwise turns and lead to painful distortions. "Failing to know God, [we] will be unable to know [ourselves], as God is the only context in which [our] being makes sense."[28] Our weekly Sabbath invitation to communion includes Augustine's invitation to "behold who [we] are, become what [we] see." In a very real way, we discover who we are in Christ the I Am.

On one level, identity is all about us, and on another it is not at all. We make choices, yes. We decide to grow or not. We act according to our values, or we don't. Yet, inherent within this autonomy, we discover that we are not, after all, "self-made" people. This kind of humility does not suggest self-abasement, just the opposite. In fact, "self rejection is the greatest enemy of the spiritual life because it contradicts the sacred voice that calls us the 'Beloved.'"[29]

The message of the Bible is that who we are matters — both personally as individuals and corporately as the People of God. Humanity, at its best, reveals something of the nature and character of God. At its worst . . . well, that comes later in the story.

---

27. David Benner, *The Gift of Being Yourself*, 47.
28. David Benner, *The Gift of Being Yourself*, 25.
29. Henri Nouwen, *The Life of the Beloved*, 21.

The search for our true selves is a lifelong, deep, and empowering quest. It involves both outer experiences and inner reflection, but unlike what others may have told you, it is not a journey to locate yourself — it is a journey to co-create yourself, to partner with God in becoming your truest self.

This is important work. People with a strong sense of self are less intimidated by others, less likely to adapt themselves to fit in, less likely to need to stand out or hide away, and more likely to speak or stand up according to their values. Our identity includes but transcends self-esteem, and it determines the esteem in which we hold others. Knowing that we are made in the image of God causes us to reflect on His being. Soon, we begin to think on things that are more noble, worthy, and full of truth. This is not to suggest that everyone with a healthy identity becomes a philosopher. Far from it. Most of us live deeply simple lives, seeking authenticity, love, and justice and finding this to be more than enough.

When we have a healthy sense of self, we are more likely to admit when we make mistakes and less likely to be devastated to discover that we are not perfect. People with a strong sense of self are more emotionally healthy and compassionate. They know that their lives matter, and they know that others' lives matter too.

Our identity began with God breathing us into life, and it continued into new life with the gift of the Holy Spirit. When we realize this, everything changes. We see that every human being has incredible, inestimable worth — both because they are human and because they are stamped with the Divine. This is what makes slavery so abhorrent and what reveals the incredible dignity and value of all human beings, regardless of how they look, act, think, or communicate. This reveals the true depths of evil in racism, colonial abuse, and exploitation. God called humanity good before we *did* a single thing. God called us good before we *achieved.*

The Psalmist reminds us that God crowns us with "glory and honor" (Ps. 8:5). Frederick Buechner muses that "the [creation] passage from Genesis points to a mystery . . . it says that we come from farther away than space and longer ago than time. It says that evolution and genetics and environment explain a lot about us but they don't explain all about us or even the most important thing about us. It says that though we live in the world, we can never be entirely at home in the world. It says in short not only that we were created by God, but also that we were created in God's image and likeness. We have something of God within us the way we have something of the stars. Life batters and shapes us in all sorts of ways before it's done but . . . I believe that what Genesis suggests is that this original self, with the print of God's thumb still upon it, is the most essential part of who we are and is buried deep in all of us as a source of wisdom and strength and healing which we can draw upon or, with our terrible freedom, not draw on as we choose. I think that among other things all real art comes from that deepest self — painting, writing, music, dance, all of it that in some way nourishes our spirit and enriches the understanding. I think that our truest prayers come from there too, the often unspoken, unbidden prayers that can rise out of the lives of unbelievers as well as believers whether they recognize them as prayers or not."[30]

At the intersection of true belonging and true self, there is a dignity that no amount of prep school, preening, or promotions could ever duplicate.

In fact, if we were to add an additional layer to the model to demonstrate what happens when our Belonging collides with our Best Selves we could visualize it like this.

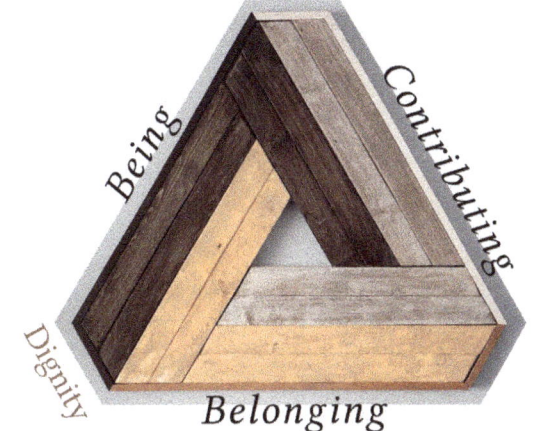

---

30. Frederick Buechner, *Telling Secrets*, 44-45.

There is an inner strength that derives from God, both within us and between us. To be made in the image of God means, among many other things, to be able to enter meaningful relationships with God, others, and ourselves. However, this is not a one-way street.

God longs for a relationship with us more than we long for a relationship with anyone or anything. We can trace God pursuing His Beloved with passion through the eons of history. This relation-

One of the most well-known parts of Michelangelo's painting in the Sistine chapel — some 300 figures painted between 1508 and 1512 — shows Adam half-heartedly reaching out to God while God reaches out to Adam (and all of humanity) with great intentionality and energy. Notice the posture of His hand on the right and Adam's on the left.

This detail of Michelangelo's Creation of Adam *is part of a larger work that covers the interior of the Sistine Chapel in Rome. Painted between 1508 - 1512. Public domain image.*

ship matters to God. Intimately engaged with every part of Creation, God's relationship with humanity is part of what links heaven and earth. There is a sense in which people, can be Thin Places — places where the veil does not seem quite as thick, and God seems closer than normal. Nowhere do we see this more clearly than in Jesus, who, fully God, took on human form to dwell among those who had forgotten whose and who they were.

We are created to Be.

To live fully.

To experience all it means to be our own self and all it means to be part of the human family.

To experiment.

To fail.

To feel.

Being made in the image of God includes both joy and suffering, both pain and pleasure.

As Thomas Merton writes, "Christianity is not stoicism. The cross does not sanctify us by destroying human feeling . . . Too many ascetics fail to become great saints precisely because their rules and ascetic practices have merely deadened their humanity instead of setting it free to develop richly, in all its capacities, under the influence of grace."[31]

I wonder: Where have I made my life small? Settled for less than the fullness available to me as one uniquely made in the image of God?

Being made in that image carries with it the responsibility to care for the things God cares for — including my corner of creation and my neighbours, especially the marginalized, and the mistreated.

Being made in the image of God also means we have been given some of God's attributes — things like creativity and the ability to think and reason. These are given so we can join God in the good

---

31. Thomas Merton, *Thoughts in Solitude*, 13.

work of creating beauty and order. Science, math, gardening, cooking, and the arts are representations of this. Every time we engage in them, we birth representations of God's abundance.

Being made in the image of God offers the humbling truth that we are called to be like God in righteousness[32] and to reflect His nature. Moreover, in the ancient world, kings were thought to bear the image of their god. To be made in the image of God is to carry the authority of royalty. Artifacts in ancient temples were also thought to represent divinity. To be made in the image of God is to carry the calling of a priest.

How do we find our true selves in this cosmic story and cast of millions? As David Benner says, "in all of creation, identity is a challenge only for humans. A tulip knows exactly what it is. It is never tempted by false ways of being . . . Humans, however, encounter a more challenging existence . . . Body and soul contain thousands of possibilities out of which you can build identities. But in only one of these will you find your true self that has been hidden in Christ from all eternity . . . as Dag Hammarskjold argues, you will never find this 'until you have excluded all those superficial and fleeting possibilities of being and doing with which you toy out of curiosity or wonder or greed, and which hinder you from casting anchor in the experience of the mystery of life, and the consciousness of talent entrusted to you which is your I.'"[33] Have you ever wondered why it seems God is chipping away so much of you? Like Michelangelo sculpting David, this is how the Artist, admittedly painfully at times, released the parts that are not us.

How do you respond to Benner's claim that our true selves have been hidden in Christ from all eternity? Does this seem restrictive or liberating to you?

---

32. Ephesians 4:24
33. David G. Benner, *The Gift of Being Yourself,* 14-15.

For me, I wonder: Where am I embracing things that may be hindering me from being anchored in the mystery of my life in Christ? This could be out of curiosity, wonder, or greed. Where am I resisting the Sculptor's chisel in favour of mediocrity? Ouch.

How can we more closely partner with God in this then? Some inner work will be necessary. Kathleen Deignan offers insight: "Contemplative life therefore begins with the recovery of one's natural unity, a reintegration of our compartmentalized, colonized, traumatized, technologically entranced and workaholic being. We must gather our fragmented selves from our distracted, exhausted, noise polluted and frenzied existence, so that when we say 'I' there is a unified human person present to support that pronoun. But that is only the preliminary work of salvation because the deep transcendent self is a divine creature, shy and wild, secret and spontaneous, preferring the silence and humility of a pure heart in which it makes its mysterious appearance. This true self must be 'drawn up like a jewel from the bottom of the sea' [she quotes Thomas Merton] by a steady work of descent to recover the immortal diamond in whose every facet is reflected the invisible face of God."[34] While this may seem like work fit only for mystics, it need not be as unapproachable as we fear. Most of us have experienced housecleaning, weeding a garden or at least tidying our desks. This is similar work. Removing the choking grime and weeds of that which is not true of us enables that which is to be more readily found.

This deep work may take us in many directions — addressing the regrets of our past and fears of our future, the expectations and assumptions we carry with us, the blinders we wear and the factors and forces that appear to be restricting our self-awareness, development and management, and understanding our true selves in our context —

---

34. Kathleen Deignan, ed., *Thomas Merton: A Book of Hours,* 25, she quotes from Thomas Merton's *New Seeds of Contemplation,* 38.

but that is the stuff of another book, a book each one of us must write for ourselves.

The journey is not merely one of self-discovery, however. The best place to start is to look at God. As Brennan Manning points out, "it is always true to some extent that we make our images of God. It is even truer that our image of God makes us. Eventually, we become like the God we image. One of the most beautiful fruits of knowing the God of Jesus is a compassionate attitude towards ourselves . . . Healing our image of God heals our image of ourselves."[35]

I wonder, in what ways is my image of God dishonouring to the Godhead, wounding to my sense of self and hurtful to the world?

May God's true self be revealed to us, so we can better worship, follow and be formed by our Creator.

Of course, knowing ourselves and accepting ourselves are two different things. No wonder this kind of inner work must be balanced by self-compassion. As Parker Palmer writes, "Self-care is never a selfish act — it is simply good stewardship of the only gift I have, the gift I was put on this earth to offer others. Anytime we can listen to our true self and give it the care it requires, we do it not only for ourselves but for the many others whose lives we touch."[36]

This need not be done in isolation. In fact, a sense of self ultimately goes beyond knowing and accepting who I am to know and accept who *we* are. In the West, we have heard, "I think therefore I am," but there are other ways of understanding this. An African Ubuntu perspective teaches, "I am because we are." Archbishop Desmond Tutu explains, "*Ubuntu* is very difficult to render into a Western language. It speaks of the very essence of being human. When we want to give high praise to someone we say, '*Yu, u nobuntu*,'; 'Hey, so-and-so has *ubuntu*.' [This means] you are generous, you are hospitable, you are

---

35.   Brennan Manning, *The Relentless Tenderness of Jesus*, 29.
36.   Parker Palmer, *Let Your Life Speak*, 30-31.

friendly and caring and compassionate. You share what you have. It is to say, 'My humanity is caught up, is inextricably bound up, in yours.' We belong in a bundle of life. We say, 'A person is a person through other persons.' It is not, 'I think therefore I am.' It says rather: 'I am human because I belong. I participate, I share.' . . . To forgive is not just to be altruistic. It is the best form of self-interest. What dehumanizes you inexorably dehumanizes me. It gives people resilience, enabling them to survive and emerge still human despite all efforts to dehumanize them."[37]

I don't want to suggest that a healthy sense of being is built on the *perception* of belonging — otherwise, it crashes when we feel excluded. Belonging is more deeply rooted than acceptance into any group. However, in a world where people are besieged with distorted versions of acceptance, we do a great thing when we make room for people as they truly are and space for whom they are becoming. This work is both sacred and unpredictable.

It can also be deeply humbling, especially as we realize how many ways of being seem foreign to us. Within the birth of human diversity is celebrated: "male and female He created them." From Adam and Eve, all the peoples of the earth are born. While we share a common identity, we are also given one unique to ourselves. In a lifelong symbol of this, we each receive our own fingerprints, uniquely stamped on us by the Creator.

Again we see this pictured throughout history and literature. Polonius's words of wisdom to his son in Shakespeare's *Hamlet* resonate still because they speak to our deepest challenge, "To thine own self be true."

In a world besieged with false versions of success and acceptance, how can we make room for contemplating who we truly are?

---

37. Desmond Tutu, *No Future Without Forgiveness,* 31.

Consider also that each human being is entirely unique. This is mind-blowing when we consider that hundreds of millions of unique individuals walking the face of the earth at any given moment. When we forget the sacredness of life, we get into trouble. When we forget our uniqueness, we also get into trouble. Every human is on a journey of self-discovery — a complex journey in which our story intersects with thousands of others and is part of God's meta-story spaning the centuries. There is great beauty in this and great mystery.

And there is grave danger when internal and external forces cause us to believe we have to live a distorted version of our true selves. We are bombarded with messages that there is one way to look, act, and speak; and many things to be owned, conquered, and achieved to be powerful and popular. No wonder so many people struggle with a false sense of self for most of their lives. It is completely understandable, but praise be to God, not irredeemable.

We are created to belong. And we are created to be our truest, God-image-bearing selves.

The lifelong nature of this quest for meaning reveals the importance of this God-given gift of identity. Signs of the journey are all around us: in the impatient stomping of a two-year-old's foot as they refuse the clothes chosen by a caregiver. A teenager experimenting with various versions of self. A person in a midlife crisis.

The quest matters. It is only as we become our truest selves that together we reveal the mystery of God in our midst. Unless we discover and become who we are designed to be, something will be missing in every space we enter. This is magnified in community. We are uniquely stamped not just as individuals but also as families, communities, organizations and nations. Living into this matters.

A godly knowing of who we are does not puff us up. It protects us. As Henri Nouwen says, "If you know you are the Beloved, you can live with an enormous amount of success and an enormous amount of failure without losing your identity. Because your identity is that you are the Beloved . . . The question becomes 'Can I live a life of faith in the world and trust that it will bear fruit?'"[38]

Our work is to rediscover the God-given dignity of humanity, the sacred beauty of diversity, and the freedom found in being our truest selves in Christ. The question, "Who am I?" is rooted in Christ and is critically important — but beyond it is a deeper and even more crucial one: "How can I live as my truest self while making room for others to do the same?"

Yet even in this, there is a danger. Our goal is not self-awareness, self-sufficiency, or centre-stage attention — although sometimes our calling may require this of us. Our goal is community, image-bearing, and fruitfulness.

For many of us, the journey towards this kind of wise, ethical, and Spirit-infused life requires the kind of inner healing and reflection that sets us free from false assumptions and lies. It enables us to break free of self-absorption, our need to be right, and our need to control. Seeing how difficult this journey is reminds us to have compassion for our fellow travellers. It helps to remember that everyone is fighting their own battle.

In my work with students, we sometimes do an exercise called the voice of the inner critic. Participants are asked to create a three-dimensional representation of the voice in their heads that keeps them from being their fullest, best selves. One day a young man we will call Chris refused to participate. He was smaller than his peers and sat off to the side through much of the retreat. Hours later, sensing someone near, I turned around to see Chris standing quietly behind me. In his hands, he held a crumpled piece of paper which he offered to me like a wounded bird. I looked at Chris. His eyes were averted. I gently smoothed out the paper to read, "puny, useless, never should have been born." The inner critic was signed "Dad."

---

38. Arthur Boers, "What Henri Nouwen at Found at Daybreak."

How can we become our full selves with the relentless warring voices that rage both inside and outside our heads? Someday this young man, or one like him, will come work for you or offer to be your friend. Be careful with the offerings being placed before you. They are often wounded and always sacred.

The fingerprint of God imprinted on us may be hidden under layers of mixed messages and shame, taking time and care to uncover. The gentle unfolding of those layers is itself a sacred calling in our shared journey to discover who we are on the earth to be, as is our willingness to accompany others on their way.

A theology of space-making leaves room for just this — for people to discover their true selves, not the version of themselves *we* want or need them to be. This is the difficult calling of parents, spouses, friends, and leaders.

I have long been fascinated that thousands of young people, in their quest for self-knowledge, come from all over the world to spend time with a Taizé monk who will listen to them. Should our youth really have to go so far to find someone who will listen? Someone who will see them?

Jesus understood just how important this is. John 1:42 records four simple words, "Jesus looked at him," yet nothing could be more profound. *Strong's Concordance* defines "looked" as to observe fixedly, to discern clearly. Peter had probably never been more "seen." We both crave and fear such knowing. One of the most touching scenes in the movie *Avatar* occurs when creatures greet each other with the words, "I see you."

Could something as simple as the way we greet one another matter so much? We live in a season where people are longing to be seen. Truly seen. How beautiful that one of God's names is *El Roi* — the God who sees me.[39] And that this name was given by an invisible woman, alone and in despair.

---

39. Genesis 16:13f

Belonging is about *whose* we are — created out of community and invited into community, we find that we are at the same time God's, ourselves', our loved ones', the crowd's, and creation's. To thrive is to live in a creation that is both glory-filled and flawed, as a glory-filled yet flawed person among other glory-filled and flawed people, with a God who is both imminent and transcendent. And to be at peace with that.

Being is about *who* we are, at our core — our character, convictions, and uniqueness. It is also about who we present to others — our strengths, weaknesses, personality, quirks, and idiosyncrasies — the parts we know about and the parts that we are blind to. It is about the gaps between our inner self and the self we offer to the world, the masks we wear and the masquerades we take great effort to choreograph and sustain to protect the tender parts of us. Perhaps that is why God speaks of a breastplate of righteousness. Our own attempts at right living and right relationships could never protect our hearts. We need the armour of Jesus's righteousness. Any other armour weighs us down, obscures, and competes.

Contributing, as we will see, is about what is in our hands. It is about the gifts we bring and how precious, or not, we understand them to be. At the intersection of Belonging and Being we find human dignity. At the intersection of Being and Contributing we will find god-honouring esteem.

Blessing:
May you truly see,
In all the ways God longs
*   for you to see.*
May you be truly seen,
In all the ways God longs
*   for you to be seen.*
May you become even more
*   fully and authentically you*
*   as you shed all you are not.*

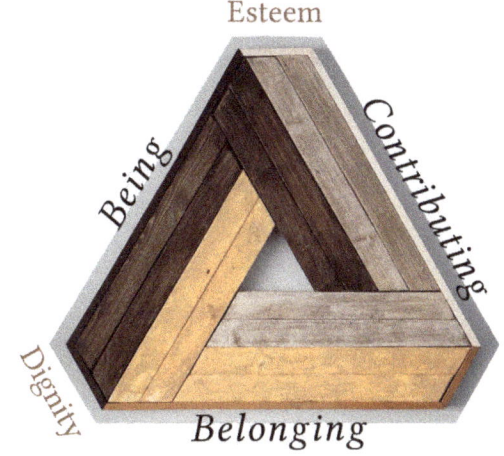

» *This section includes its own tension of being-becoming. Do you tend towards contentment with the way you are or stretching towards growth? In what ways does that affect you? (both positive and negative)*

» *Knowing whose voice to listen to is deeply important. How has God's voice shaped your sense of identity?*

» *Have you made your life smaller than it could be or larger than it should be in any areas — resisting the Father's chisel in favor of mediocrity or other unhealthy motivations?*

» *How do you respond to Benner's quote that our true self has been hidden in Christ from all eternity?*

» *Where are you embracing things that may be hindering you from being anchored in the mystery of your life in Christ?*

» *How has your worldview shaped your identity? Do you relate more to "I think therefore I am" or "I am because we are"? Why?*

» *How are you intentionally making space for others to grow into their God given true selves?*

» *There is a natural tension between being and contributing that we could describe as being vs. doing. How is that playing out in your life?*

Contributing

OUR EMERGING SENSE OF SELF leads naturally to experimentation. We try new things — discarding some as not for us and adopting others as areas of interest and ability. We begin to act and observe how our actions affect us and others.

In ancient Hebrew thinking being, and doing could not be separated. In the West we tend to think of these as distinct, often stressing to people that we should not define ourselves by what we do. For the ancient Hebrews, it made sense that what you do and what you say flow out of who you are, and that who you are is influenced by what you do. As we transition into considering the third piece of God's ideal for thriving humanity it is with the knowledge that all three are deeply connected and interdependent.

It is also the place of another creative tension. On the one hand, we are fully loved and fully human before we can contribute in any meaningful way. On the other, the opportunity to contribute is hugely important to our sense of belonging and identity. To be deprived of this opportunity robs us of fullness. One might even argue it robs us of part of our humanity.

In the Genesis 1 creation account, God blessed humankind, saying, "Be fruitful and multiply and fill the earth and subdue it and have dominion over it." We are given a task, a calling, a job. This work is set in the context of a garden, and throughout scripture, we find contribution framed by the language of fruitfulness. John 15:16 picks up the metaphor — a helpful, seasonal perspective in our productivity-focused world that I admit to struggling with. In John, Jesus was angry with a tree that did not bear fruit. "This fig, lush with leaves, was barren of fruit. In other words, it had been hoarding all its resources for itself. Its mission had become to look good more than to feed a hungry world and a hungry Messiah . . . when God said 'be fruitful and multiply' the Lord was only calling us to reflect God's nature. God is fruitful and multiplies. The fertility of the universe is amazing . . . when God commanded the first Adam to till and tend the garden and to 'conserve and conceive,' God was giving humans their prime directive. We were put here not to consume but to conceive. Jesus confronted a culture of consumption, reflected in the unproductive fig tree, with a culture of conception. 'Every good tree bears good fruit.' . . . 'You will know them by their fruits' . . . Jesus called His disciples to be more than faithful — He called them to be fruitful." Similarly, "cruelty and cupidity are not what the Creator had in mind when entrusting humans with dominion over creation. This is made clear at the end of the story when part of each person's divine judgment includes the question: How have you cared for the earth? (Revelation 11:18)."[40]

God's idea of dominion is stewardship, not ownership or ruler-ship. Jesus expands this, saying the "rulers of the Gentiles lord it over them . . . it shall not be so among you."

We have seen that by creating us out of loving community and calling us into loving community, we are given the opportunity for rich relationships with God and each other. By creating us in His own image, God gives us the opportunity for a loving relationship with *ourselves.*

Now we discover that by creating us to contribute, God also invites us into loving relationship with the rest of creation. We are given the opportunity to enjoy, enhance, create, care for, steward, shepherd, use wisely, breathe our lives into, cultivate and bless the very universe that God loved enough to build.

In the incredible kindness of God:

We are created to Belong.

We are created to Be.

And we are created to Contribute.

---

40. Leonard Sweet and Frank Viola, *Jesus: A Theography,* 42-43.

Without meaningful contribution our lives quickly narrow to boredom, illness, or distortions of fullness. I am not just talking about paid work, as important as that might be, or even about volunteering or hobbies. I am talking about that piece we alone bring to the table; the calling that is upon our lives, that unless we find and do it, may go undone. The passion or anointing we bring into any room with us, that we may undervalue because it comes so easily, but that represents something deeply significant about God's heart for the world. What do you carry with you? Peace? Mercy? The ability to mobilize people? The ability to bring order out of chaos? This unique ability is part of your makeup and is important in understanding your unique contribution to the world.

Through this lens we see that discussions of work-life balance can lead to unhelpful binary thinking. Anyone who owns a home or is a parent or spouse or friend knows how much work is needed to steward these well. We also do inner work. We work out our faith. We work at our hobbies and fitness. We work at what matters to us. In some cases reframing our conversation with questions can be helpful.

Questions like:
Where are the spaces I want to do my best work?
How will I ensure I show up in those spaces ready to bring my best?
What do I uniquely bring wherever I go and where is that most needed right now?
How does my paid work allow me to bring my best to other spaces?

What can I do about the ways I sense my paid work detracting from my ability to do good work in other important areas? Without this perspective, our paid work can become an idol or a curse — a soul-crushing pursuit of productivity, performance measures and possession. Or it can lead to silent resentment, regret, and wracking disillusionment. God help us from living in, or creating, these places of toil. To be proud of our work is light years away from being proud in our work. Service is on the opposite side of the galaxy from being a slave to our jobs.

The mindset of contributing can be both personal and communal and it is rooted in our worldview. Original peoples of Mexico "practice *tequio*, the voluntary gifting of work and time . . . for the sake of the collective good. In Mali, *dama* is a pay-it-forward practice of keeping gifts on the move, circulating continually through the community . . . Among Native American communities of the Pacific Northwest, the potlatch is a festival in which wealth is redistributed through reciprocity; the status of a family is determined not by how much is owned but by how much is gifted to others. In India, *sewa* is a spirit of selfless service, performed without any expectation of reward or gain. And the list goes on. *Butsu Butsu* in Japan. *Susu* in Trinidad and Tobago. The *Kula ring* in Papua New Guinea. *Aropa* among some Pacific Islanders. *Barn raising* among the Amish."[41] These perspectives offer a fresh lens through which to view contribution — especially to worldviews steeped in consumerism and transactional exchanges.

We receive glimpses of the joy and dignity of work in God's original ideal. The telescoped story of Adam and Eve's creation is retold in more detail in Genesis 2. God placed the man in the Garden of Eden "to work it and keep it." Yet on Adam's first day on the earth, eager to please God and get going, he discovers that God's seventh day, is a day of rest A day of blessing and holiness. I imagine Adam settling in to learn the heartbeat of God in this wonder filled place.

There was no disparity to God. In the Hebrew language work and worship derive from the same word. Worship is the work of God's people just as work can be an act of worship to God. This is reflected

---

41. Margaret Wheatley and Deborah Frieze, *Walk Out Walk On,* 141.

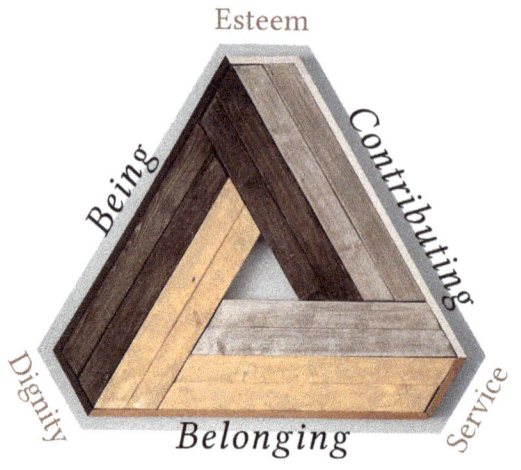

Esteem

Being

Contributing

Dignity

Belonging

Service

True service, motivated by love and utilizing our unique contribution, is found at the intersection of Belonging and Contributing, and with it comes another great gift.

in the Hebrew language. The phrase *Avodat Elohim* refers to the work, worship, and service of God.

And here is another unexpected twist. Our work, in all its unfolding and nuanced manifestations, is God's gift to us — given so we can know Him, become our true selves, and connect with creation in meaningful ways. It is not something we do for God. It is something God does in us.

That may sound lofty. I speak as a privileged, white woman. As Patrick Reyes explains, in circles like mine we think of vocation as "God calling us out of our present reality and into some divinely purposed and infinitely better future . . . In fact, God often just calls us to survive."[42] Commenting on this same thought Kat Armas adds: "This is true for most people in the world; their Christian calling is simply survival. When we talk about vocation in privileged spaces, we forget that surviving . . . is holy too — a sacred endeavor."[43]

Work and dignity are closely linked. Rabbis often plied a trade. Paul was a tentmaker. Jesus was a carpenter. Work has sacred meaning. I learned this on a retreat. Upon arrival at the Abby in Iona, I discovered that everyone is given a daily task. Mine was to dry the dishes after breakfast. On the first day, I picked up a towel and went

---

42. Patrick Reyes, *Nobody Cries When We Die* (Chalice Press, 2018) quoted in Kat Armas, *Abuelita Faith*, 186.
43. Kat Armas, *Abuelita Faith*, 186.

to work. Halfway through the task, halfway through drying one cup in fact, the bell rang, signalling time for prayers. Rushing to finish the cup I felt a gentle hand upon mine and turning saw one of the Anglican nuns smilingly but firmly indicating that the cup could wait. We entered the sun-drenched sanctuary and settled into the times of music, prayers and silence. When the bell rang again everyone stood but I, feeling myself both more spiritual and more in need than the rest, wanted to sit for a few minutes more. I felt a gentle hand on my elbow and opened my eyes to see the same nun, smiling but insistent again. It was time to work. Back and forth between the two expressions of faith we moved, like waves going in and out; each complemented and depended on the other. To work without worship was lifeless to worship without work was to miss the partnership of co-care and co-creation God offers. This same pattern, marked not with bells but with sunsets and sunrises, was established from the very beginning.

Showing up for his first day of work Adam, discovered that you rest with God before working with God. He should have known, "there was evening, [*then*] there was morning, the first day." Days began with sleep and ended with work. Since Jesus's resurrection, our week begins with rest and worship. Chronic Fatigue Syndrome taught me the hard way what God wanted me to know all along. Rest first, then work. Trust God first to go ahead of you into the day, then work. Worship God first, then work. Pray first, then work. These are all expressions of *Avodat Elohim*, and to neglect one is to miss the whole point.

Then Monday comes. We stand with Adam, ready to learn the next important lesson. It is subtle but significant. The same verbs of "working and keeping" found here (or "tending and stewarding" in some translations) are used elsewhere of the priests' work in the temple. Stewardship is a sacred calling. It is not until Genesis 3 that work become toil. In Genesis 2 work is still filled with discovery, joy, and bounty.

Seeing the fruitfulness of the earth, Adam perhaps begins to understand the fruitfulness that is possible for himself. Seeing the diversity of creation, perhaps he wonders how he can ever possibly name each creature the Lord brings to show him. As beautiful as the surroundings are and as fulfilling as the work, it seems it is not sufficient for Adam. There is too much to be done for one man. There is no one like him to talk or laugh or cry with. Adam feels alone.

The Community of God understands and says, "It is not good for the man to be alone" (Gen 2:18). So God creates for him an *ezer* (as we have seen, this suggests a strong helper — language used elsewhere of God's help to humanity). Adam, in the third poem of the account, welcomes Eve with joy, as if the first human interaction is too profound to leave to prose. Reflecting on this passage raises questions for me. How did God experience this first human conversation? Did creation still as the community-born-from-community first interacted? Did Adam fall to his knees in wonder? Did Eve look first at Adam or at God?

Eve was given as companion and co-worker, a helpmate in the great work of stewarding Creation. We are not meant to do the work alone. Nor is working a human-only endeavour. Jesus came saying, "My Father is working until now, and I am working."[44] Together we join God in work that is already in progress.

There is something inherently good about this. We sometimes read Romans 8:28 to mean, "for those who love God all things work together for good." However, N.T. Wright and others have argued that the original text suggests it is not the things that work together but God and His people who do! We could say that God works (from the word *sunergeo* — from which we get "synergy") with and through His people for all things to become good. Now that is worth reflecting on.

This kind of work is, not surprisingly, a labour of faith and love. Paul picks up this theme in 1 Thessalonians 1:3 when he describes the

---

44. John 5:17

people's "work of faith and labor of love and steadfastness of hope." Faith and love take work. Work takes faith and love. And work needs strong helpers.

Like Adam and Eve, we are created for community, and it is for and out of community that our best work emerges. Of course, bringing value *through* our contribution is not the same thing as finding our value *in* our contribution. We are wise to learn how to differentiate what is motivating and life-giving from what is insidiously dangerous to others or destructive to us. This may be harder than it sounds. The culture around us celebrates productivity, prestige and popularity. God calls us to contribution, being and belonging. These are not at all the same thing.

In fact, Psalm 127:2 warns us that, "It is in vain that you rise up early and go late to rest, eating the bread of anxious toil; for He gives to His beloved rest." The beloved do not live by Genesis 3:19, we live by Psalm 127:2. Jesus came to redeem all things. Thriving involves the integration of work and rest, sleeping while God works for the first half the day, then joining God in the work given to us for that day; re-creating and re-connecting on the first day of the week so we have life to bring with us into the other six days.

Luke tells the fascinating story of Jesus healing on the Sabbath. He restores a man's withered hand.[45] The main point of the story is that Jesus is Lord of the Sabbath, a day intended for redemption, not rules. However, there may also be a subtle and counterintuitive subtheme. With a withered hand, the man's work would have been impaired. On the Sabbath, Jesus gives him rest from his *inability* to contribute. Jesus's focus is always *Shalom* and Sabbath is meant to be a weekly glimpse into this multifaceted, life-enhancing, Divine gift.

The same redemptive view applies to raising children. Psalm 127:3 goes on to remind us that, "children are a heritage from the Lord, the fruit of the womb a reward." The labour of childbirth we read of in

---

45. Luke 6:6-10

Genesis[46] becomes a reward in the hands of the Redeemer. Work inside or outside the home is valuable in God's kingdom. This is echoed in the English word economic which is made up of two concepts:

eco (household) + nomic (care for)

True economics means caring for — not charging for.

Of course, contributing is not the same as perfectionism or people pleasing, by choosing (or using) our work to appease. Nor is contributing the same thing as overachieving, work-a-holism, or conversely, getting by with as little effort as possible. Overachieving is one of the greatest distortions of our opportunity to make a difference in the world. It begins young and comes with a devastating cost. *The New York Times* published an article on high-achieving, ambitious girls and their "jam-packed schedules," amped up multi-tasking and "profound anxiety." One mother expressed concern that the obsession with achievement could lead to "anorexia of the soul."[47] The definition of aimlessness is to be without purpose or direction. The result of over-activity is depletion, not completion. God's ideal for our purposeful work is that it feeds our soul, not starves it.

We have seen that God's idea of contribution is a labour of love, best envisioned as fruitfulness, not productivity. We join our Father who is always working, but also knows the importance of Sabbath.

Still, our work can be tied to our sense of worth in both healthy and unhealthy ways. Many people struggle to see value in the work they view as mundane, or they resist taking on new challenges due to low self-esteem. Throughout scripture we see many examples of people fearful to take on the assignment God offers them, and only a few who answer, "Here I am Lord, send me."[48] I am fascinated by the promise given to sceptics and believers alike, as God said to Gideon,[49]

---

46.   Genesis 3:16
47.   Sara Rimer, "For Girls, It's Be Yourself, and Be Perfect, Too."
48.   For example, Mary the Mother of Jesus (Luke 1:38) and Isaiah (Is. 6:8)
49.   Judges 6:14-16

Moses,[50] the disciples,[51] and us — "I am with you." Contribution collides with belonging in this promise. Of course it does, for they are
closely linked. Paul reminds us that whatever we do should be done
with thanksgiving and in the name of Jesus.[52] He also teaches us that
our best contributions will be gift-based not talent-based, and in a full
circle moment, done in love.[53]

Work can give our lives tremendous meaning. Visionary architect
and thinker, Buckminster Fuller, when depressed and contemplating
suicide is said to have asked himself two questions that revolutionized
his life. "What is my job on the planet? What is it that needs doing,
that I know something about, that probably won't happen if I don't
take responsibility for it?"

I developed a fresh appreciation for the importance of purposeful work during the Covid-19 pandemic. On the days I did not have
something interesting to put my mind to or something physical to
exercise my body, I found the isolation and uncertainty much harder.
I should point out that this was not always paid work. In fact, for part
of that season I was laid off. Praying more deeply for our world, for
example, was, I believe, not only important in the heavens but also
profoundly powerful in helping me meaningfully navigate that time.

Many of us struggle with knowing what we could do, especially
against the seemingly insurmountable challenges of our world. Sometimes the deepest wisdom comes from unlikely places. In a folktale
from China, called "Holding Up the Sky," a hummingbird is lying on
her back, feet in the air, when an elephant comes along and asks what
she is doing. The hummingbird explains that she heard that the sky is
going to fall and is ready. Scoffing loudly the elephant asks what such
a tiny creature could do to hold up the sky. The hummingbird explains

---

50. Exodus 3:17
51. Matthew 28:20
52. Colossians 3:17
53. 1 Corinthians 13

that she doesn't plan on doing it herself, but she is willing to do her part. The elephant thinks for a moment, and then lays down beside her and puts his feet in the air. Sometimes the smallest contributions on our part can trigger significant change.

One time a young woman named Eva attended a series of leadership retreats we were hosting. Observing her sleep through every session I asked her teacher about it. "If you knew about her home life you would understand why. She only sleeps where she feels safe," she explained. Thankful that we could at least provide her with rest, we let her be. On the final day of the final retreat as we went around the circle sharing what we had learned we came to Eva. I expected her to ask for a pass. Instead, she quietly said, "I am not saying that I think I am a leader, but I have learned that if I did think of myself as a leader that could change everything." Sixteen other, normally rambunctious students, sat silently as the power of those words descended upon us.

We have a voice. We have a job. We bring a unique contribution. Just like our sense of belonging and being, it may be hidden under layers of hurt. The unfolding of those layers is itself a sacred calling in our shared journey to discover what we are on the earth to contribute.

Mary Oliver asks in her poem "The Summer Day":
> Tell me, what is it you plan to do
> With your one wild and precious life?

Our work is to choose gift- and passion-based service over:
- aimlessness (lack of clarity about what to do)
- laziness (lack of motivation)
- unhealthy overwork (working to prove to or hide from ourselves or others or work that is expected of us by others rather than gifted to us by God)
- toil (work that does not bring life) or
- taking advantage of those under our influence (the coercion or literal or figurative enslaving of others)

This is harder than it sounds. Our work, parenting, purchasing, and communication practices must be examined in this light.

Work is not always pleasant or "nice." It may include confronting, taking risks, and, almost always, making sacrifices. Even when we approach it with a redemptive mindset and passion our work may be hard and seemingly thankless. It still has meaning.

Counter-intuitively, our work can also involve waiting. In fact, waiting may be one of the most difficult works we do. Waiting for a loved one to be ready, waiting for a child to develop in a womb, waiting for God's timing on a project . . . waiting can be pregnant with anticipation and promise, and calls out the best of our hope and faith. Waiting invites us into the mystery that is going on beneath the surface and beyond our realm. Waiting transforms and transcends for "unless a seed dies and goes into the ground . . . "

While the Hebrew people waited for 400 years, God was silent but at work. While the angels watched, Mary awaited the arrival of the Messiah. While creation held its breath, Jesus' body lay in a tomb. Then with unprecedented power, rocks, religions, and realities split in two. Resurrection.

Waiting occurs for individuals and communities. Sometimes for nations. During the pandemic, the world waited. Nowhere is the work of waiting more important than in cultural transformation. For what is culture after all? In Latin, *cultura* means a cultivated land. We are back to the concept of fruitfulness, with seasons of labour and of waiting.

Most counter-intuitively of all — and here is where our triangle becomes cyclical — our greatest work is to love. We have discussed doing our work with love. Colossians 3:23 reminds us that our work is one of the ways we honour and love God. Jesus takes this even further, saying: "This is my commandment, that you love one anoth-er."[54] Our work is to be done in love. Our work *is* to love.

---

54. John 15:12

If we remember nothing else, remember this: God is our Beloved and the purpose of our life is to learn to love well.

Any labour that is not done in love has little to no Kingdom meaning. Any task accomplished for its own sake is lifeless. Any act, even of justice, forgiveness or restoration, not surrounded by love, is self-seeking. Only that which flows from the Circle Dance we call the Trinity holds the seeds of the New Creation.

This is why John reminds us, "Little children, let us not love in word or talk but in deed and in truth."[55]

And this is why our core question is not "What should I be doing?" but "How can we do this with love?"

This raises questions for us. Where are the gaps and inconsistanties? How can I serve with love?

As friends, parents, spouses and leaders, the corollary question will by now be obvious. "How can I make space for others to serve with love?" This may mean stepping aside from our own beloved project. It may mean stepping in to clear a path. Most often it will mean listening.

We cannot leave this section without raising one last thought. In the footsteps of the Suffering Saviour, we find that, in ways too mysterious and painful for us to understand, even suffering finds a place here — bearing the fruit of which we catch only glimpses.

Miroslav Volf reminds us that, "Jesus' greatest agony was not that he suffered . . . [it] was the abandonment."[56] The passion of Jesus not only purchases our salvation but also ensures that no one is ever alone in suffering again. Solidarity. Presence. Even when He seems distant.

Counterintuitively, James 1:2 invites us to consider it all joy when we meet trials of various kinds. For, in echoes of the language of *shalom*, trials enable us to to be perfect, complete, lacking in nothing.

---

55.   1 John 3:18
56.   Miroslav Volf, *Exclusion and Embrace*, 26.

Suffering is the pathway to wholeness.

At the intersection of contributing and belonging another creative tension exists.

Rooted in Belonging, we must still release our grasp of it to develop our otherness.

Rooted in Being, we realize that while we have nothing to prove there is still much to be done.

Rooted in Contributing, we discover that only by abiding can we experience true fruitfulness.

Again and again. Around and around. Being filled and pouring out.

God's ideal for humanity.

Prayer: "Jesus has the power of God, by which he has given us everything we need to live and serve God. We have these things because we know him." 2 Peter 1:3

> *May we walk in the freedom and power He provides,*
>   *serving Him out of love.*
> *We are created to Belong, to Be, and to Contribute.*
> *This is what Thriving looks like.*
> *This is Abundant Life.*
> *This is Shalom.[57] To be restored and made whole.*
>   *To partner with God in the good work of reconciliation,*
>   *redemption and restoration.*
> *This is a picture of homecoming, gathered around*
>   *the table of God as "chosen, holy and beloved"[58] ones.*

---

57. A Hebrew word meaning peace, wholeness, completeness and well-being, perhaps best captured in the words "nothing broken, nothing missing."
58. Colossians 3:12

» *This section includes the tensions of God working through us and our working with God, work as service for God and work as God's gift to us, inner work and outer work. Are you experiencing any of these tensions at this point in your journey?*

» *How does thinking of contribution as fruitfulness rather than productivity shape your thinking?*

» *How does thinking of contribution as paid and unpaid work and hobbies — and also the God given gift that you knowingly or unknowingly bring into the room with you — shape your thinking and actions?*

» *Reflect on your work as something to be done with love and your work as to love. What insights do you see? Do you agree that the core questions are not 'what should be done' or even 'what should I be doing' but 'how can this be done with love' and how can I make more space for others to serve with love?'*

» *Reflect on how not being able to contribute robs us of part of our humanity. Are there any spaces where you are sensing this in yourself or others around you? How could you more intentionally create spaces for people on the margins of your work to contribute to it?*

» *What insights do you see in N.T. Wright's interpretation of Romans 8:28?*

» *As we come full circle to consider the relationship between contributing and belonging, we discover that this is the place of service and it is also the place of creative tensions. Supporting vs. enabling. Giving vs. receiving. Clan vs. culture. Are you currently experiencing any of these tensions? How are you navigating them?*

2

God's Ideal Repeated
— In the Language and Lessons of Covenant

BELONGING, BEING, AND CONTRIBUTING are deeply woven into the Creation story, as we have seen. They are also foundational to God's covenantal relationship with humanity.

Covenants serve as the backbone of the biblical story, linking Adam,[1] Noah, Abraham, Moses, David, Jesus, and God's people in a thousands-of-years-old unfolding of relationship and responsibility. In Old Testament times, covenants were binding promises with far-reaching implications, far beyond our current idea of contracts or commitments. They link us to God and each other in powerful ways reminiscent of adoption and inheritance. The closest version we have is marriage — when entered willingly, intending to honour the other. In fact, the language of marriage — found in the opening and closing chapters of the Bible and most explicitly in the Song of Solomon — best enables us to understand the kind of relationship God offers as our Beloved bridegroom.

The Song of Solomon is a book unlike any other in the Bible. Some suggest it offers a poignant retelling of Adam and Eve's story. Placed

---

1. While the word covenant is never mentioned, many scholars believe the elements of covenant are embedded in this story, providing a jumping-off pad for the covenants of love that God establishes with humanity from the beginning to the end of time.

again in the wild cultivation of a garden, a man and woman emerge. Hiding is replaced by discovery, "I found him whom my soul loves,"[2] shame by wonder, "I am very dark but lovely, O daughters of Jerusalem,"[3] and toil with pleasure, "King Solomon made himself a carriage . . . its interior was inlaid with love."[4]

In an interesting twist that could easily be lost in the scope of the story, Solomon's beloved is transformed by his presence, saying, "I was a wall . . . then I was in his eyes as one who finds peace."[5] Love knocks down our walls. Love changes us. Love changes everything.

The book hangs upon the recurring refrain, "I am my beloved's, and my beloved is mine," and this heartbeat drums through the centuries as our deepest longing — like the iconic line in the film *Moulin Rouge,* "the greatest thing you'll ever learn, is just to love and be loved in return."

No wonder so few preachers teach from this text. It is raw, real, and easy to spiritualize away. Yet here it is in our Bibles, even in the King James. What are we to make of it? If covenants are the backbone of the Bible, surely the Song of Solomon is its heartbeat. Pulsing back to the writings of David, echoed in the words of the prophets,[6] and saturating the gospel and letters of John with the language of love, commitment and devotion. Beloved-ness is also the life-blood of the covenants, hidden in words like loving-kindness, everlasting, chosen-ness . . . and even jealousy.

God established a covenant with Noah, repeating the language of Creation by saying, "be fruitful and multiply and fill the earth . . . God made man in his own image . . . Behold, I establish my covenant with you and your offspring after you, and with every living creature that

---

2. Song of Solomon 3:4
3. Song of Solomon 1:5
4. Song of Solomon 3:9-10
5. Song of Solomon 8:10
6. See, for example, Isaiah 5:1

is with you,"[7] and setting a rainbow in the sky to commemorate the event.

God's covenant with Abraham promised "an everlasting covenant to be God to you and to your offspring after you."[8] Rooted in a deep relationship between God and Abraham's descendants, it offered the people a unique identity, ultimately connecting family and homeland with the promise of a son and a nation.[9] It also provided a method for God and mandate for His people, to bless the whole earth while acting with righteousness and justice.[10]

Belonging. Being. Contribution. On a national scale.

As a side note to this story, I am fascinated by the fact that Abram "listened to the voice of Sarah," reminiscent of Adam listening to Eve. Both Adam and Abram heard directly from God, but they quickly were swayed by another voice. This challenges me deeply.

Reading on, we see God was personally available to listen to Hagar, the mistreated servant of Sarah.[11] And He gave her a covenantal-like promise in poetic language (Genesis 21:18), foreshadowing that of Mary, the mother of Jesus (Luke 1:31-33).

When God restated the Covenant with the newly renamed Abraham, He ensured that Abraham knew the covenant included Sarah saying that she would "become nations" and "kings of peoples would come from her."[12]Adam and Eve. Moses. Abraham and Sarah. Hagar. David. Mary. Covenanting with God. Belonging. Being. Contributing.

God used Moses, the Law, and the time wandering in the wilderness to teach Israel how to be the people of God, saying, "I will take you to be my people, and I will be your God."[13] Belonging. As Moses

---

7.   Genesis 9: 1-9
8.   Genesis 17:7
9.   Genesis 15:1-21
10. Genesis 12:2, 18:19
11. Genesis 16:7-14,17:20
12. Genesis 17:16
13. Exodus 6:7

said to the people: "what great nation is there that has a god so near to it as the Lord our God is to us . . . ?"[14] This story points to the unique offer of adoption into God's family. Moses asks, "has any other god ever attempted to go and take a nation for himself from the midst of another nation . . . because he loved your fathers"[15]? This relationship changed the people from everyday folks to God's "treasured possession," a "kingdom of priests," and "holy nation."[16] Identity. It also came with a calling — to walk in God's ways and bless their neighbours. Contribution.

As they did this important work, three things would happen:
1. Their nation would be healthy and their leaders wise.
2. They would be respected by, and able to bless, the nations around them.
3. Other nations would see that God was with them and honour God.

We see this enacted in Judges 4. God used Deborah and a military victory to enable her people to refocus their identity from *"the people of Israel"*[17]— living in the fearful shadow of a ruthless neighbour — to *"the people of the Lord"*[18] living in freedom under the shadow of God's wing.

One of the most beautiful examples of this kind of covenantal love is found in God's relationship with David. We often hear of the shepherd-boy-made-king's heart for God. Equally powerful is God's faithful heart for David. David wanted to build a house for God. In

---

14. Deuteronomy 4:7
15. Deuteronomy 4:34-37
16. Exodus 19:6
17. Judges 4:1
18. Judges 5:11

language reminiscent of the Father in the Prodigal Son story, God insisted on building a home for all His children instead.[19] God creating a home for creation, promising Abram a family, bringing the Israelites into the Promised Land, calling Deborah a mother in Israel,[20] promising a house for David, setting the lonely in human families[21] and people in the family of God, Jesus promising the Father's house has many rooms[22] . . . throughout all of these, we can see this promise to David as part of an unfolding invitation to come home.

Sadly, David squanders resources and responsibilities in actions reminiscent of the Prodigal Son. Yet he was forgiven. Therefore, David was able to truthfully say, "I will sing of the steadfast love of the Lord forever; with my mouth I will make known your faithfulness to all generations . . . You have said, 'I have made a covenant with my chosen one; I have sworn to David my servant.'"[23] He had experienced first-hand the unconditional, forgiving, second-chance-giving steadfast, loving-kindness of God. No wonder so many of David's psalms flow from his understanding of what it means to be loved with covenantal *hesed*.[24]

Generations later, when speaking of the restoration of Israel, God promises again: "you shall be my people, and I will be your God."[25] In fact, the language of belonging permeates God's promises: "I have called you by name, you are mine. When you pass through the waters, I will be with you... you are precious in my eyes and honoured, and I love you . . . I am with you; I will bring your offspring from the east, and from the west, I will gather you. I will say to the north, Give up

---

19. 2 Samuel 7:1-11
20. Judges 5:7
21. Psalm 68:6
22. John 14:2
23. Psalm 89:1-3
24. Loving-kindness
25. Ezekiel 36:28, see also Jeremiah 30:22

and to the south, Do not withhold; bring my sons from afar and my daughters from the ends of the earth . . . whom I formed and made."[26]

This new covenant will be written on people's hearts, for, as God insists: "I will be their God, and they shall be my people."[27] This new covenant would be ushered in by a chosen servant, One in whom God delights. One who would establish justice on the earth and come as a light to the nations,[28] bringing an eternal covenant of peace and charging God's children with a renewed call to steward and care for the earth. For, "the covenant-call to be God's people, far from being primarily an invitation to special privilege, is, first of all, a summons to special responsibility. God calls a people to live in response to the needs of others, to live in right relationship with God, to bring justice and mercy to the land, and to lead the way towards peace and freedom."[29]

Reflect on that language for a moment.

Eternal

Covenant

Peace

Justice

Freedom

Light to the nations

Now *that* is surely something worth giving your life to partner with God for.

Enter Jesus and the world-shaking gift of a new covenant offering a place of true belonging, a foundation for our re-envisioned identity

---

26. Isaiah 43:1-7
27. Jeremiah 31:33
28. Isaiah 42: 1-7
29. *Seeking God's Peace in a Nuclear Age,* Ronald E. Osborn, ed. as quoted in Reuban P. Job's *A Guide to Prayer for All God's People,* 183.

and partnership with the Divine. The writer of Hebrews 8:8-12 quotes from Jeremiah 31, applying the promise of a new covenant written on people's hearts to Jesus. Hebrews announces Christ as the Way to God and the way to be the people of God. In a previously unfathomable manner, the Divine-human relationship is both embodied and offered. All the promises are now realized in Jesus, who describes a massive family homecoming saying, "in My Father's house are many rooms."[30] At the Last Supper, He explains how this is possible, saying, "This is My blood of the covenant, which is poured out for many for the forgiveness of sins."[31] Then, in a poignant and powerful moment on the Mount before returning to the Father, Jesus pleads with us to join Him in gathering the family home. Notice the promise Jesus gives for this heightened partnership: "Go therefore and make disciples, of all nations, baptizing them in the name of the Father, and of the Son and of the Holy Spirit . . . behold I am with you always, to the end of the age."[32] Homecoming. Many rooms. Forgiveness. With you always.

This is the Good News retold. The New Covenant, paid for at a great price by Jesus, purchases for us the opportunity to live out God's Creation ideal — to be redeemed as the Beloved.

- Belong. Through Jesus, we are offered deep relationship with God, each other and ourselves.[33] Amazingly, God opens the Godhead community to invite us in, and within this sacred space, we find ourselves.
- Be. Through Jesus, we are redeemed of our old nature and given a new, holy, true one.[34] Now seen by God in and through Jesus, we are set free to be our truest, best selves. God shares

---

30. John 14:2,3
31. Matthew 26:28
32. Matthew 28:18
33. John 15:9-17
34. Matthew 26:26-28

His identity with us while simultaneously partnering with us to co-create our most unique selves.

- Contribute. Unbelievably God includes us in the Divine work. He entrusts to us the things that matter most to the Father, Son, and Spirit and invites us to create with the kind of resources and license few artists, inventors, or innovators ever have. "Now may the God of peace, who brought again from the dead our Lord Jesus . . . by the blood of the eternal covenant, equip you with everything good that you may do His will."[35]

What is it we are building? A new Kingdom as God's Beloved people. God loves us with everlasting love. The depth of this is perhaps nowhere as clearly as in the symbolism of communion. One Bread broken for one body, and One Body broken for one bride.

In communion, we are bound to the Trinity and to each other, our personal and corporate identity is confirmed, and we enact the fulfillment of the purposes of God. No wonder communion is such a sacred and important embodiment of the Jesus-loving community. However, we cannot appreciate it fully without understanding the dark side of this story.

---

35.   Hebrews 13:20-21

3

The Opposite of God's Ideal
– Living as the Betrayed

GOING BACK TO GENESIS, we pick up one chapter later to see the devastating effects of the distortion of God's ideal.[1] Looking around we see it in ourselves and our world.

There is a telling progression to this fall. First, Adam and Eve listen to the wrong voice. Then they worry they are missing out on something. Guided by their senses rather than God's instruction, they take what is not rightfully theirs. Shame enters their experience, and Adam and Eve's first response is to hide. Lacking the courage to confess what they have done, they turn to blame. They have forgotten whose they are and in so doing, lost themselves.

Reading the story, I also wonder, how does the writer of this account know *me* so well?

Author and Spiritual Director Jan Richardson suggests a provocative, alternative reading of this passage. She asks, "what hunger caused Eve to reach for the apple? . . . Within her gesture lies the impulse that would animate the restless searching of all the following generations."[2] She ponders if perhaps Adam and Eve's greatest sin was not in the taking but in the hiding, in the distancing of themselves from the only One who could set things right.

---

1. Gen. 3
2. Jan Richardson, *In the Sanctuary of Women*, 29-32.

Who among us cannot relate?

The quest may take us to strange places. As Annie Dillard suggests: "At the heart of my resistant longing for God is the knowledge that to call upon God, to cry out, as did the prophet Isaiah, 'Oh that you would tear open the heavens and come down!' means giving myself to the prospect, the surety, that God will draw me out to places from which I can never return."[3]

Exploring what other, less traditional themes might be hidden in the story, Richardson reflects on Adam and Eve clothing themselves in fig leaves, saying, "What if it wasn't their shame that drove them to garb themselves but rather their beauty? What if seeing each other with eyes wide open was too overwhelming to bear? To fully see and be seen is dazzling. And fearsome . . . Thomas Merton once wrote, 'There is no way of telling people that they are walking around shining like the sun.' Yet, as he knew, to make the attempt is part of our wondrous and terrible vocation. In this broken world, we are called to open ourselves to the beauty that persists. To allow ourselves to see, [to be seen] and to be stunned."[4]

Whatever the mix of motives and emotions, sadly, in poignant poetry, we read that Adam and Eve's relationship with God and each other became tainted, their identity marred, and their connection to their work changed forever. Ever after, they will live partially hidden — disconnected from God, creation, and themselves — and afraid.

In their own children, Eve and Adam see the fruit of their actions. What parent among us cannot relate? The story is peppered with the language of connectedness. The word "brother" appears seven times, for this is a story about relationships; it is a story about family. The first family in fact, and the first human opportunity to partner with God to create spaces for genuine belonging. I think it is safe to call this first attempt a massive failure.

---

3. Annie Dillard, *Teaching a Stone to Talk*, 40-41, as quoted in Jan Richardson, *In the Sanctuary of Women*, 34-35.
4. Jan Richardson, *In the Sanctuary of Women*, 38.

Eve names her firstborn Cain, saying, "I have gotten a man."[5] It is a full circle moment — as God made woman from man, now God makes man from woman. The narrator acknowledges the intimacy required between Adam and Eve for a child to be conceived and Eve acknowledges her partnership with God for a child to be born.

Belonging. Interdependence.

There is hidden theatre in Cain's name and it suggests he may have had more than one choice available to him. In Hebrew, it can mean *acquire*, as in something we gain through purchase. This is the way it is normally translated and described, suggesting that commercial and consumer mindsets have already replaced God's invitation to stewardship. However, the name can also mean something that is created or that grows, like a tree that "acquires" its branches. His name is also related to a Hebrew word that means *spear*, and others that suggest *weaving* and *lament*. Weaving as a bird weaves its nest with its beak, and lament as a poem or prayer that pierces our soul like a spear. Contrary to what I believed for years, I now believe that Cain had choices. A metaphorical spear was put into his hand at birth, and like us, he had the choice of how to wield it.

God warns Cain, "sin is crouching at the door and its desire is for you." Ignoring the promise that "if he does right he will be accepted," Cain opens the door, and sin leaps in. Why did Cain murder his brother? We read that he was angry. Angry at God, perhaps? Jealous of his brother? Disappointed in himself? Disillusioned with the land he loved and confused about the Divine work he had been given? Whatever the alchemy of reasons, having forgotten whose he was, Cain forgot who he was, and did what he never dreamed he would do. He killed his own brother. Disconnected from God, his family, and his home, Cain becomes disconnected from himself, wandering as a

---

5. Gen. 4:1

fugitive on the earth. With one hateful choice and an unwise response to it, Cain lost his family, his place, his self-respect, and his life purpose.

We may be tempted to get stuck wondering why Cain's offering was not sufficient. This is not the point of the story. The point of the story is that God offered Cain and now offers us the chance to ask, "What offering would You have me bring? How can I ensure that both my offering and the way that I bring it are honouring to You and respectful of my brothers and sisters? God show me *my* contribution and help me to bring it out of love, not vanity, comparison or fear."

The point of the story is also that relationships are fragile. They can be sacrificed, at great cost, out of insecurities that simmer beneath the surface then strike with force. God protect us from the darkness that causes us to forget whose and who we are.

Cain and Abel were brothers. There is only one person in the Bible named Abel, Eve and Adam's second child. In Assyrian, his name means *son*. In Hebrew, it means *breath*. God breathed life into his body. Sadly, Cain snuffed it out.

Cain had seven generations of offspring, but his lineage ended at the flood. None of us are the descendants of the murderer Cain. Neither are we descendants of the victim, Abel. We are all children of Adam and Eve's long-living son Seth, whose descendent Noah walked with God. We do not have to follow in Cain's footsteps.

Yet sadly, so many do. . .

If we flip the thriving model on its head, we see the reality that many experience.

Instead of belonging, so many in our world experience *alienation.*

This shows up in different ways. Co-dependence, shallow or shattered relationships, estrangement, power differentials, fear, loneliness, and hatred replace healthy friendships, families, and communities. Whether our estrangement is self-imposed or imposed upon us, the results can be devastating.

Instead of being their true selves, so many hide behind distortions.

Disguising ourselves, we are tempted to settle for spaces steeped in part truths or shame and manipulation. Like navigating a carnival House of Mirrors, this journey can be confusing and exhausting, leaving us with limited resources to find a way home to ourselves.

Instead of meaningful work, so many become trapped in toil — a spectrum of responses from aimlessness to TGIFs, from striving to wastefulness, from workaholism to overworking others for our benefit, and, taken to the extreme, to slavery. This is no labour of love. This is exhausting, entangling, and life-sucking toil. And it is hard to avoid. Almost every first-time conversation begins with "What do you do?" and every family or work gathering involves the celebration of someone's achievement or the veiled discussion of someone's failures or procrastination. The messages we receive from birth include: we are what we achieve, we are what we have, we are what scores we get or goals we master, and we are valued according to how much we line up with what others call success.

Nothing could be further from God's ideal.

While the first triangular model represents what it means to live as the Beloved, the bottom paints a picture of *the Betrayed*. While the top offers *shalom* the bottom is a picture of the slippery slope to the emptiness and despair of *sheol*. A place without true love or life. *Shalom* is the place of sons and daughters, *sheol* is the place of slaves. *Shalom* is the place of equity and justice, *sheol* is the place of discrimination and abuse.

Problems arise when any one of these areas are distorted or when we try substituting one for another. Seeking to fill the emptiness of loneliness with work; hiding our sense of inadequacy behind unhealthy relationships; abdicating responsibility because of selfishness or fear. Settling for idols.

There is a world of difference between the work, worship, and service of God (represented in the top model) and the work, worship and service of idols. We may recoil against the thought of idol worship yet be unknowingly trapped in self-olatry, spouse-olatry, child-olatry, work-olatry, newest stuff-olatry, shopping or other addiction-olatry, or even ministry-olatry.

Esteem

Being · Contributing

Dignity · Belonging · Service

Alienation

Hiddenness · Slavery

False-self · Labour

Hopelessness

Note how the meaning and abundance released when our true selves align with our true calling are degraded into poverty and hopelessness when the false self meets toil. Poverty can take many forms: financial, social, and spiritual — and it causes downward spirals that can be complex to reverse.

When we bring our true selves into places of belonging, there is communion and dignity. Contrast this with the cruelty and hidden-ness found at the intersection of our alienation and false selves. We have heard it said that *hurt* people *hurt* people, and this can be true. It is equally true that hidden people can make themselves seen in unexpected ways.

Sit for a moment with the despair felt by an abandoned toddler, a chronically bullied teenager, an estranged father, or a betrayed woman. Allow the weight of it to sink in. That is what alienation feels like. Multiply that now across countless faces.

We are getting to the good part. I promise, but first . . .

Imagine the desperate measures we take to break free from this quiet desperation. We will do almost anything to find someone who will accept and "love" us. No wonder we change ourselves to fit in. No wonder we do things we never thought we would. No wonder we ruminate over regrets and angst about the future. Our relationships — with God, ourselves, others, and the world — are all broken.

We spoke earlier of the four kinds of relationships included in community. We can redraw the model to show the effects of sin brokenness. Each of the relationships is profoundly influenced. We could diagram this as follows:

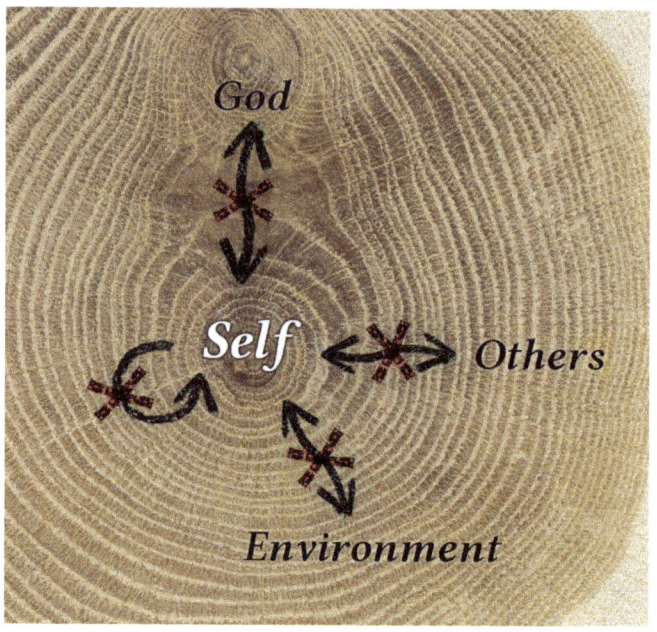

No wonder we feel so alone.

Much of our personal and social angst stems from this sense of alienation, a disconnection from our heritage and traditions as well as our neighbours and extended families. A professor of psychology, Dr. Jean Twenge says, "Anxiety increases as social bonds weaken. Societies with low levels of social integration produce adults prone to anxiety."[6] Her research demonstrates that a lack of social trust is the highest predictor of anxiety, higher than divorce, economic conditions or unemployment rates.

---

6.   Quoted in "Social Bonds," *Crown Me With Love Blog*, May 2017. See also, Geoff Mcmaster, "Millennials and Gen Z are more anxious than previous generations: here's why," *University of Alberta: Folio,* Jan. 2020.

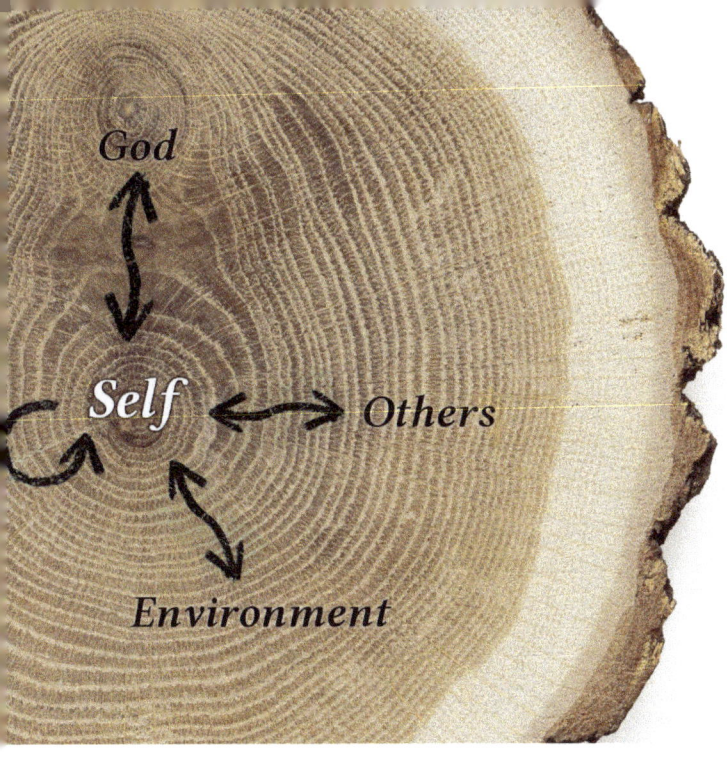

God

Self ←→ Others

Environment

The Great News is that Jesus came to restore all of these relationships.

Yet, we settle for less.

This does not necessarily mean that full restoration occurs instantaneously. Sometimes God frees and transforms us immediately. More often, this degree of redemption is possible only as we partner with Jesus in the work of healing, reconciliation, renewed mindsets, and changed behaviour needed for us to live in *shalom* with God, self, and the rest of creation.

This is not lost time. This is an important life-quest time.

The Bible is filled with wanderers and exiles: Abram and Sarai, Jacob, Moses, Naomi and Ruth, the Israelites in the desert, Mary and Joseph, Paul, and Jesus. In the wilderness and the wayside, they meet with God who is everywhere and makes every place sacred.[7] As we learn from the arc of all great myths, our travels can transform us, going out in one state and returning in another, either with gifts for the community — as in the story of Moses — or with the awareness of our need for the gifts of community — as we will see in the story of the Prodigal Son.

———————

7. See, for example, Jeremiah 29:11-12

As a result of our brokenness, our identity is also threatened. Rejection shames us into hiding, lying, blaming, and making ourselves small. Losing sight of the glory and possibility of being truly ourselves, we drift into some version of a false self — crafted knowingly, or more often unknowingly, to protect ourselves from further hurt or so we can fit in somewhere. Co-dependent relationships, gangs, and unhealthy marriages can stem from this unmet need. So can many other unhealthy survival techniques and "acting out" behaviours.

In an interesting study of what motivates us, Daniel Pink suggests that there are three key factors: purpose, personal mastery, and autonomy. I add belonging to this list. The fascinating thing about these motivators is that when we become disillusioned, we protect ourselves by going in the opposite direction. Someone who is idealistic and highly motivated by purpose, once wounded, may become a skeptic. Someone wired to excel may become complacent and de-motivated. Someone who can truly think alone and outside the box may develop learned helplessness to protect themselves from further hurt. And someone who highly values relationships and mutual respect may turn to anti-social behaviour in an "I-am-going-to-reject-you-before-you-can-reject-me" kind of way. How then are we to interact with the skeptic, the complacent, the one who pushes others away? According to who they are, not according to who they are presenting to be. Yet, we do not often remember this, and thus the patterns reinforce. We get defensive ourselves and soon forget who *we* truly are.

Psychology, sociology, and anthropology all document how dangerous and pervasive such distortions can be. When we seek our identity in being popular or intelligent or hard-working; or when work-a-holism or laziness impacts our family or team; when we seek to compensate for our fears through control or perfectionism; or when we believe we have to wear masks or follow the crowd in unhealthy behaviours in order to be accepted; these are methods of survival, not thriving.

The temptation to hide is massive — going back to Adam and Eve in the garden — and it is reflected in every word, and deed humanity has done to protect itself. We are terrified to be ourselves because we fear there is nothing of value under the surface after all.

Perhaps this is why, as Thomas Merton explains, "Every one of us is shadowed by an illusory person: a false self. This is the person that I want myself to be but who cannot exist because God does not know anything about him. And to be unknown to God is altogether too much privacy. . . Thus I use up my life in the desire for pleasures and the thirst for experiences, power, honour, knowledge and love to clothe this false self and construct its nothingness into something objectively real. And I wind experiences around myself and cover myself with pleasures and glory like bandages in order to make myself perceptible to myself and to the world as if I were an invisible body that could only become visible when something visible covered its surface."[8]

This often leads to comparison with and imitation of others who seem to be getting it more "right" than I am. Yet, as "Rabbi Zusya, when he was an old man, said, 'In the coming world, they will not ask me: "Why were you not Moses?" They will ask me, "Why were you not Zusya?"'"[9]

How then can we heal from the painful layers of scar tissue that build up over time in our inner core? The apostle John is once again our guide. It is only as we immerse ourselves in the unconditional love of God that we are able to more fully love and receive love. Love truly does cast out all fear. Our journey is not towards people pleasing, perfection, and productivity. Our journey is towards loving relationships, self-differentiated selves, and fruitfulness.

We repeat then. If the top triangle represents what it means to live as God's Beloved, the bottom is surely what it means to live as the Betrayed.

---

8.   Abridged excerpt from Thomas Merton's *New Seeds of Contemplation*, 29-36.
9.   Peter Scazzero, *Emotionally Healthy Spirituality*, 89.

If the top triangle is a picture of *shalom*[10] on earth, the bottom must be a picture of *sheol*.[11] One the picture of a life cherished and well lived; the other of fear, deterioration, and destruction.

We see these same three perversions of God's best offered by Satan to Jesus in the wilderness. They are carefully wrapped in the guise of goodness.[12] The first two of the temptation accounts begin with the words, "*If* you are the Son of God." Satan is tempting Jesus to disbelieve or to prove, His Sonship and identity — whose He is and who He is. This same temptation can be traced through history and be seen in our own lives. A constant but subtle bombardment of messages that we do not belong, that God does not truly love us, and that we are not enough. No wonder it takes faith to believe. No wonder we find relief in putting others down to make ourselves feel better. No wonder we fight. We need transformation.

In the first temptation, Jesus is offered what He naturally craves after forty days of fasting — food. He is also offered the chance to show what he can do and solve the problem of world hunger. Who among us would not love to do that?

In the second temptation, Jesus is taken to the pinnacle of the temple in the holy city and asked to prove himself by jumping. What a fast tracked way to prove His divinity. Yet, Jesus did not jump. He knew He had nothing to prove and nothing to gain from stepping outside the timing and ways of His Father. How often I *have* jumped, forgetting these very things.

In the third temptation, Jesus is offered the kingdoms of the world in exchange for worshipping Satan. Jesus responds, "Be gone, Satan, for it is written: You shall worship the Lord your God and him only shall you serve." In a full circle way, Jesus reminds us that we belong to the Father, our identity is grounded in Him, and we are to bring our

---

10.   A Hebrew word meaning peace, wholeness, completeness and well-being, perhaps best captured in the words "nothing broken, nothing missing."
11.   The place of darkness and death.
12.   Matthew 4:1-11

best contribution to Him alone. *Avodat Elohim* not *avodat elillim.*[13]

In his writings, Henri Nouwen described the three leadership temptations he saw in this text as the temptations to be relevant, spectacular, and powerful. "'I will give you all the kingdoms of this world in their splendour,' the demon said to Jesus . . . One of the greatest ironies of the history of Christianity is that its leaders constantly gave in to the temptation of power . . . even though they continued to speak in the name of Jesus, who did not cling to his divine power but emptied himself and became as we are. The temptation to consider power an apt instrument of the Gospel is the greatest of all."[14]

Why is this such a great temptation? Nouwen explains that "success, popularity and power can indeed present a great temptation, but their seductive quality often comes from the way they are part of a larger temptation of self-rejection. We have come to believe in the voices that call us worthless and unlovable, then success, popularity, and power are easily perceived as attractive solutions to our desolate condition."[15] Which temptation is most alluring to you? Nouwen offers three alternatives for leaders:

To model integrity.

To give followers a place to belong.

To give followers authority to act.

Nouwen's alternatives sound a lot like the three parts of our model. Jesus truly is the Way. Betrayal can be experienced both personally and corporately. "Absence of shalom and lack of harmony are expressed in social disorder as evidenced by economic inequality, judicial perversion, and political oppression and exclusivism... These offenses are viewed by the prophets not simply as ethical violations but as disruption of God's intention for shalom."[16]

---

13. Work, worship and service of God, not of idols.
14. Henri Nouwen, *In the Name of Jesus*, 75-76.
15. Henri Nouwen, *Life of the Beloved*, 21.
16. Walter Brueggemann, *Living Towards a Vision*, 18.

» *This book uses the language of living as the Beloved for the first triangle and living as the Betrayed for its inverse. Does this language resonate with you? Why or why not?*

» *Jan Richardson asks, "what hunger caused Eve to reach for the apple?" What hunger do you think it might have been? What hungers are you experiencing that may be causing you to look in the wrong places or reach for the wrong things?*

» *Is alienation from others, distortion of your God created self, or exhausting toil affecting your soul? In what ways is this impacting you?*

» *How do you see alienation from others, distortion of their God created self, and exhausting toil affecting the soul of your community? What insights do you see in this?*

4

God's Ideal Restored
– In the Language and Lessons of the Christ

IN MATTHEW, WE READ THAT upon seeing the great crowds, Jesus went up on a mountain and sat down. The disciples came to hear what they knew He was preparing to say. They must have been deeply confused by His message. Two thousand years later, readers still are.

We have been raised to believe that to be blessed is to be loved, accepted, and valued. To be blessed is to have privilege and power. To be blessed is to have health and wealth. To be blessed is to grow up as the beloved child of a prosperous parent, attend the best school, get a good job, live in a peaceful neighbourhood in a peaceful nation and pursue what matters to you. To be one of the "haves" in a world of "have nots." How relatively easy it is for healthy, privileged people to experience *shalom*. How unfair for everyone else.

What then of those less fortunate? What of those born to parents who are struggling, raised in neighbourhoods of want, or those who don't fit in at whatever school they attend? What of those born with health issues? Those whose innocence is stolen? What of the disillusioned and betrayed?

Walter Brueggemann reflects on this saying, "People who live in the midst of precariousness shape their vocabulary and their faith . . . in a distinctive way. One of the most important ways the Israelites expressed their faith was around the theme of 'cry out, hear and deliver'. . . Israel is a people who cry out. Yahweh is a God who saves

... the conclusion is a theology of salvation."[1] For those "whose life is not precarious," the concerns are less urgent and more proactive. They become "questions of proper management and joyous celebration. . . [resulting in a] theology of wellbeing. . . a theology of blessing."[2]

People who suffer tend to go in one of two directions. They become hardened or compassionate. It is easier to become hardened. People who are fortunate also tend to diverge into those who feel entitled and those who are thankful and generous. It is so easy to slip un-intentionally into entitlement.

Jesus quietly explains a third way. Superimposing those who have with those who have not, He explains there are people who are bless-ed, who may be rich in money but poor in spirit, who suffer yet are comforted, who don't wait in vain for the inheritance that will be theirs, who turn pain into mercy, who when surrounded by iniquity still become pure or when bombarded with violence still live in peace. In Jesus's upside-down kingdom it is not where we have come from or what we have experienced that determines which version of the triangle we live in; it is something else. And to find it usually takes a journey.

For our 40th wedding anniversary, my husband and I travelled to Ghent, a bucket list destination for me. This spectacular city show-cases stunning Medieval architecture and houses the 15th Century masterpiece known as the Ghent Altarpiece. The survival of this mas-sive and breathtaking painting — believed to have been completed by Hubert and Jan Van Eyck in 1432 — is nothing short of miraculous.

---

1. Walter Brueggemann, *Living Towards a Vision*, 28-29. See for example Ex. 2:23-25, 3:7-8, 6:5-6; Ju. 2:18b, 10. 12b,14; 1 Sam. 7:8-9.
2. Walter Brueggemann, *Living Towards a Vision,* 30-31. See for example Gen. 1:31; 8:22; 2 Sam. 7:15-16; 1 Kings 4:20; Deut. 33: 27 and contrast with Psalm 90:1-2.

Facing Page: The Ghent Altarpiece, *or* Adoration of the Lamb. *Painted by Jan van Eyck in 1432.*

The panels were almost burned by rioting Reformers. They were stolen by Napoleon. Finally recovered and restored, the painting was then stolen so often during World War II — before being rescued by the infamous Monuments Men — that it is believed to be the most frequently stolen painting in history. One panel is still missing despite a concentrated decades-long attempt to recover it.

Many art critics agree that it is also one of the world's most influential paintings. As the first major oil painting, it serves as a visual representation of the storyline of the Bible and insight into the theology of the day. This unprecedented scope is matched only by its incredible realism and detail. Centred around a large panel called the *Adoration of the Lamb,* the altarpiece, when opened, features Adam top left and Eve top right. Above Adam's head, Cain and Abel make their offering to God. Above Eve Cain murders his brother. Deliberately shocking in contrast, it provokes us to self-reflection. As I stood mesmerized by the panels, I gradually realized that I was not examining the painting; God's Spirit, through it, was examining me.

The New Testament parable of "The Prodigal Son" is believed by many to be a redemptive retelling of the Cain and Abel story. It opens with the words, "There was a man who had two sons." This code-like invitation encourages us to think of Cain and Abel, Isaac and Ishmael, and Jacob and Esau. However, as the story unfolds, the youngest son turns out not to be productive like Abel, trusting like Isaac, or clever like Jacob. This young man is irresponsible, thoughtless, and self-indulgent. He scorns his home, identity, and calling, throwing them away with apparent abandon. Having forgotten whose he was, he forgot who he was and therefore squandered all he had on scandalous living. Who cannot relate on some level? Betrayed into thinking this was the life he wanted, he betrayed all he most loved and all those who most loved him.

This story's beautiful turning point comes when the young son "comes to himself." As if waking from a horrible nightmare, he remembers who his father is. He has learned what Thomas Merton will later pen, that "the one thing above all others in importance is to return to the Father." This prompts him to recall all that he had at home, remember who he is, and consider all he longs to be. I imagine the son reflecting on the dignity of the simple work they did on the farm and the lavish meals and laughter around the family table. Remembering, he turns away from what has become distasteful and starts the journey home. If you know the story, you know that the father — who by now we can call our Father — picks up his robes and runs to greet the boy, joyfully dismissing his request to work as a servant and fully restoring him as his beloved son. Lest we are tempted to think this paints a picture of some future place in the heavens, we recall that God's new Kingdom has already begun on earth, that the Son returned to His home on earth and went to work — as can we.

This is the ultimate story of family & homecoming — "*you are not going to the pig pen; you are coming in for a feast!*"

It is the ultimate story of the restoration of identity — "*you are not strangers or slaves; you are my sons and daughters!*"

It is the ultimate picture of life purpose, as the son, who by now we realize is us, is given the authority to get things done — "*take off these rags and put my robe and rings upon him.*"

And what of the older son? He is also a prodigal, even though he lives and works in his father's house. He has his version of entitlement and disillusionment. He also is us. And his is the saddest story of all, for nowhere do we read that he also "came to himself." Cain famously asked, "Am I my brother's keeper?" The older brother in this parable demonstrates similar disdain. The story is left deliberately unfinished. Perhaps so we can finish it ourselves.

Certainly, the question "who is my sibling or neighbour?" is an important one for us. Layering the stories of Cain and Abel, the Prodigal Son, and the Good Samaritan, we see that the one who loves God knows the answer. Our neighbour is whoever God places in front of us.

How do we love them? The one who journeys with God discovers the answer. As we adopt more and more of the Spirit-given attributes of the Beloved, our fear-based jealousy, selfishness, and tendency to compare begin to fall away. We become increasingly meek, merciful, pure in heart, living as righteousness-craving, poor-in-spirit peace-makers. We become the Beloved children of God.

The Prodigal Son is the culminating story of the trilogy of Lost and Found parables recorded in Luke 15. While perhaps the best known of the three stories, it is not meant to be read alone. It is powerfully portrayed in Rembrandt's famous painting by the same name.

The shepherd in the painting has eyes only for the sheep. His fingers clutch the side of the abyss. On his knees and at great risk to himself, the shepherd reaches out to the helpless creature.

Parable of the Lost Sheep, *by Alfred Usher Soord. Painted in 1898 or 1900. Public Domain image.*

Parables are more complex than allegories. They are designed to provoke us into new ways of thinking and acting because they speak to our deepest longings, showing us where these align (or don't) with God's heart. Parables transcend time because they can be read through many personal, cultural, and theological lenses. For our purposes we will read them through the lens of Genesis 1:26-28.

The three parables respond to the complaint that Jesus is eating with undesirables — people considered non-neighbours. Non-brothers. Jesus is crossing cultural norms in a big way, and the conservatives present do not like it. In ancient times, eating together had almost covenantal implications — it was a big deal. Jesus responds to this complaint with three stories.

In Luke 15:3-7, we read Jesus' first parable. This "Parable of the Lost Sheep" is captured by British painter Alfred Usher Soord (1868-1915) in his most famous work.

The question that sparked Jesus to tell these three stories suggested Jesus was compromising Himself and undermining the community. Here we see that the opposite is true.

The parable is powerful on so many levels. It shows us:
- how far the sheep has wandered and the extreme trouble it is in as a result
- the lengths the shepherd will go to bring the sheep back into the fold
- the importance of our work as under-shepherds following in the footsteps of the Great Shepherd

Matthew's version of this story contrasts sharply with a time and culture where it was customary for unwanted children to be neglected. It is these "little ones," and all other most-vulnerable human beings, that the shepherd goes out of His way to find.

The reason? "I tell you that in heaven their angels always see the face of my Father who is in heaven . . . it is not the will of my Father who is in heaven that one of these little ones should perish."

You may know first-hand the panic of a toddler gone missing in a mall. Or you may carry that piercing sadness of an estranged teen. As we multiply that feeling thousands of times over, we begin to sense the pain in the heart of the Father as He looks upon the plight of humanity.

Of course, the lost-ness we are referring to here goes far beyond geography. We can easily be lost emotionally, spiritually, and socially. We can be lost from ourselves as well as from God or others. Jesus speaks to every part of us as He invites us home. And He calls on His followers to go searching for their lost brothers and sisters; to create spaces where they will find welcome; giving the incredible promise that "whoever receives one such child, in my name, receives me!" It is no accident that Matthew begins by introducing us to Jesus as Immanuel — God with us — and closes with His words, "I am with you always, to the end of the age."

This is the encircling message of the Good News — God is among His people via Jesus and the Holy Spirit. God has made His home in our midst so we can be at home where we are.

The sheep in this story was well and truly lost. Our kids are growing up in a society that craves genuine belonging yet experiences cyberbullying, loneliness, and disillusionment with parents, politicians, and prayer. No wonder so many feel alienated.

However, it is not just our kids who are struggling. It is easy to lose track of whose we are, who we are, and why we are here in the relentless task of keeping work, family, neighbours, friends, and even places of worship safe and satisfied. In this story, the shepherd heart of God comes looking for us.

In Luke 15:8-10, we find the next parable in the Lost and Found trilogy. The Parable of the Lost Coin is captured in a painting by the well-known French Impressionist James J. Tissot, who lived from 1836 - 1902.

The Lost Drachma, by James Tissot, 1886-1894. Watercolour over graphite. Currently on display at the Brooklyn Museum. Public Domain image.

The woman represents the mother heart of God. Separated from God, we have become separated from ourselves. Forgetting our imprint, we have forgotten to whom we owe allegiance. But the mother heart of God has not forgotten us. In Isaiah 49:15, God promises, "Can a mother forget her nursing child. . . even these may forget, yet I will not forget you."

The inciting question presumed that Jesus did not know with whom He was associating. His stories demonstrate that nothing could be further from the truth. He saw their external flaws. He chose to remember their deeper identity. This is the same way He looks at us.

His gaze is revolutionary and transformative in a world besieged by superficiality and judgment.

Our kids are struggling, growing up as they do in a society that has forgotten what it means to be fingerprinted with God's glory. We are struggling, seeking to live into this truth. I wonder to myself, "How can I live my life, so this is more often on display?"

The realities of our world are taking their toll on human beings. We live in an age of increasing expectations and diminishing resources. With the ever-present realities of war and pandemics that spread at lightning speed, we wrestle within a rapidly changing world, where decision-making, trust building, and community spirit are increasingly hard to navigate.

In Industrial England, miners sent canaries down the shafts ahead of them to test the air quality, knowing that these tiny birds were more sensitive than humans and would be more reliable indicators of healthy conditions than their own lungs. Today, many individuals and families, our current day canaries, are struggling – indicators of systemic societal overload.

Perhaps you also have lost track of whose you are, who you are, and why you are here in the seemingly limited resources and limitless needs that surround you. In the parable of the Prodigal Son, the Father heart of God comes looking for us.

The parable we mentioned earlier is captured in Dutch master Rembrandt's final and most famous oil painting, *The Return of the Prodigal Son*. This version was probably completed within two years of his death in 1669. It represents countless hours of meditating on the story and years of living into its mysteries.

The first time I saw a Rembrandt painting, I unexpectedly burst into tears. It was not this one but the massive and spectacular *Night Watch*. Something about it spoke deeply to me, and I have been fascinated by Rembrandt ever since. Considered one of the greatest storytellers in the history of art, Rembrandt was an acute observer of

The Return of the Prodigal Son. *Rembrandt van Rijn, 1661-69. Water-colour over graphite. Currently on display at the Hermitage Museum, St. Petersburg. Public Domain image.*

humanity and a master of light and shadow. Perhaps it is this juxtaposition that shows us so much of ourselves when we immerse ourselves in his work.

This painting is not the only version of this parable that Rembrandt completed, but it is the one that so poignantly demonstrates that the painter has come to understand the tender heart of God. Dressed in luxurious robes, he nevertheless clutches the long-lost son to himself. No questions are asked. Rembrandt beautifully captures how light, shade, shadow and darkness; longing and lost-ness; intimacy and jealousy play against each other in this story.

Henri Nouwen has written powerfully about this painting. According to him, one of the Father's hands is larger and rougher than the other. On the young boy's shoulders sit both the Father and Mother hands of God. Perhaps less well known is the fact that before seeing the original, Nouwen meditated on a copy for three years and worried that seeing the real painting might be a disappointment. "The opposite was true. Its grandeur and splendour made everything recede into the background and held me completely. Coming here was indeed a homecoming,"[3] he later said.

As we have seen, not only is the son invited to a feast but he is also given a task, symbolized by the robe and ring. It is time to take up his rightful place as a son, and with that comes responsibility.

In fact, this parable is the penultimate story of:

A welcome home

A restoration of our true identity

An invitation to return to our life purpose

The questions that prompted Jesus to tell these three stories also suggested that the people had forgotten who and what mattered.

A shepherd hanging off a cliff. A mother on her hands and knees.

---

3. Henri Nouwen, *The Return of the Prodigal Son*, 8.

A father running down the road. This is the God of the universe we serve.

In our world, we can know everyone without knowing anyone. Know a little about a lot. Feel part of without *being* part of, or be part of without feeling it.

Shallow or digitally enhanced relationships, busy schedules, and urban living all contribute to a disconnection from people and place. No wonder our kids are struggling. No wonder we are. Into this culture, the Father-Mother heart of God runs towards us, inviting us to come home.

A trilogy of lost and found stories.

A trilogy of redemption.

Three living pictures of God's heart for humanity.

As such, it is also a three-pronged reflection of:

- what it means to thrive
- how far God is willing to go to give this incomparable gift
- what our collective work really is

Together they paint the picture of our true twofold calling — to create places where all people, young and old, can thrive; and to actively seek out those who have lost their way and point the way back home.

The New Testament is filled with redemptive retellings.

Jesus engaging with the woman at the well — perhaps the first man to speak to her without lust, disgust, disdain, or pity. He was the one who gave her back community, dignity, and a meaningful calling. Belonging, Being, and Contributing replacing fear, abuse, and shame.

Jesus setting a child in their midst and calling him great.

Jesus giving daughters and sons back to fathers and mothers.

Jesus describing a Samaritan as an example of a godly neighbour.

Jesus choosing a blind man to show others how blind they are.

Jesus feeding the five thousand and turning the tables on any who would take advantage of those without.

Who is at the centre of all these retellings? Jesus.

Jesus is continually eating with the poor, touching the leper, and speaking to the outcast, for Jesus is ushering in a New Kingdom. In the tension of what theologians call the "now and not yet," our thriving is restored. Yet, still to come, the brokenness within and between genders, generations, socio-economic classes, differing physical and mental capacities, races and ethnicities, leaders and followers, perspectives and preferences, and most of all, families and communities, now all with the possibility of redemption. No more lording over or living in shame. No more need for alienation, false selves, aimless-ness or toil. In their place, Jesus offered *shalom*. And He gave Himself so we could have it.

Hebrews 12:18-24 emphasizes this saying, "For you have not come to what may be touched . . . But. . . to the city of the living God . . . and to the assembly of the firstborn who are enrolled in heaven, and to God . . . and to Jesus the mediator of a new covenant, and to the sprinkled blood that speaks a better word than Abel." Jesus, the Living Word, setting all things right and inviting us into an eternal family.

Here is perhaps the most outstanding part. God through Jesus *gives us* peace, and God through Jesus *is* our peace.[4] No more "us and them." No more "outsiders and insiders." All the dividing walls have been broken down. All of them.

This is the story of homecoming.

Zacchaeus coming down from the tree to take Jesus to his home.

Mary and Martha making a home away from home for Jesus.

Jesus ensuring a home for his mother from the cross.

The church birthed as a home for the Spirit and for us.

Jesus, putting Himself on display so we could see His Father.

Jesus going to prepare a place for us in His Father's House.

---

4. Ephesians 2:14, Judges 6:23-24

Our calling is to make a home for each other, and for Him, in our hearts, work, and families.

In the beginning, God, dwelling within the Trinity and understanding the power of Love, knew it was not good for us to be alone. Therefore, God invited us into the Divine Circle Dance and placed us in human communities.

In the beginning, God stamped us with the Divine image and then painstakingly individualized us so profoundly that everything we touch leaves our own distinctive fingerprint.

In the beginning, God created a cornucopia of nature's richness and gifted us with the purposeful work of stewarding the earth, learning from our shared past and co-creating our shared future.

In the covenants of the Old Testament, God bound the Divine to the finite, promising a level of relationship and partnership unheard of in any other era or setting. By wandering in the wilderness with Moses, by waiting under a date palm with Deborah, through the laments of the prophets and in the hope-filled songs of worship of the Psalms, God emerges as the One who longs for a people to love.

In the New Testament, these seeds explode with fresh meaning. It is almost impossible to imagine all that God has done in Jesus for us.

Through the disobedience of a man and woman, evil and death entered Eden. Through the obedience of the Son of Man, righteousness and life return in full. "For our sake, he made him to be sin who knew no sin, so that in him we might become the righteousness of God."[5]

Through the murder of a brother, the ground was stained. Through the sacrifice of a Brother the stain is washed away. For Jesus is "the mediator of a new covenant," and His "sprinkled blood" is a "better word than the blood of Abel."[6]

Redemption.

---

5. 2 Corinthians 5:21 ESV
6. Hebrews 12:24 ESV

Redemption is Love in action, Love pursuing us, reminding us, inviting us. For: "Love invites all to the dance of freedom, to sing the Beloved's song of truth. The voice of Love strikes with fire upon hearts of stone. The voice of Love uproots the thorns of fear, Love uproots fear in every open heart. The voice of Love is heard in every storm and strips the ego bare; and in their hearts all cry, 'Glory.' The Beloved lives in our hearts, Love dwells with us forever."[7]

As this prayer suggests, the metaphor of God as a loving Father-Mother welcoming us home is incredibly powerful and transformative. It is a picture of safety, nurture, and intimacy. In fact, the Bible offers a variety of metaphors representing the levels of intimacy people can have with God. We could draw these as a pyramid with the Potter and clay metaphor at the bottom.[8] This understanding is critical for us. God is the potter, and we are to be responsive clay. The Bible also teaches that God is the Master, and we are His slave/servant.[9] Our understanding of lordship is crucial to the discipleship process. But Jesus also says that He no longer calls us only servants; he has called us friends.[10] To be a friend of God is an amazing invitation and something that will take a lifetime to explore. Yet there is more!

While sadly, we rarely dare to imagine just what this means God offers to be our Loving Father.[11] To truly believe that we are children of God is an incredibly important step in our faith journey.

However, a child's relationship to a parent is not the same as the almost embarrassingly intimate and intriguing picture of Beloved and Lover. This is suggested in places like the Song of Solomon and 1 Thessalonians 1:4. One could argue that this is presented in the Bible as the

---

7.   Nan Merrill, *Psalms for Praying*, 49.
8.   Isaiah 64:8
9.   Romans 6:21,22
10.   John 15:15
11.   1 John 3:1

highest level of intimacy a follower of Jesus can have with God. Lest we dismiss this as something only for a few, it is essential to recall that "the family is the dominating metaphor used for the church all throughout the Second Testament . . . the bond of which was shared divine life. This brings us back to God's eternal purpose, which is to obtain a bride for the Son, a house for the Father, a body for the Son, and a family for the Father."[12] Why would we settle for less?

Living as the Beloved changes us.

Loving the Beloved changes everything.

As Nan Merrill so eloquently writes:

"Blessed are you who reverence the Beloved,
who walk in Love's way!
You radiate an inner joy and peace
Whe'er you go;
Compassion draws you to the gates
Of those in need.
Families and friends gather
Upon your doorstep;
Children run to greet you
With open arms...
Strangers feel at home
In your presence;
The oppressed are comforted
By your support.
Blessed indeed are you who reverence
the Beloved.
Peace is within you."[13]

---

12. Leonard Sweet, *Jesus: A Theography*, 148.
13. Nan Merrill, *Psalms for Praying*, inspired by Psalm 128, 263-264.

Jesus is the living, breathing embodiment of what it means to live as the Beloved. He is the Second Adam who came to redeem all that was broken in the fall, demonstrating this in His life and making it available to all who would believe in His death and resurrection and the gift of the Holy Spirit. He is the embodiment of the New Covenant, as His name Immanuel suggests, He is "God with Us."

These themes are picked up in the book of Hebrews. Jesus is introduced to us as God's Son.[14] His abiding sense of belonging grows from a deep awareness of His Sonship.

In Hebrews 1:3, we read that "He is the radiance of God's glory and the exact imprint of His nature." Jesus' understanding of His identity is crafted by His complete trust in being stamped with the imprint of God. God's glory is His essence, sometimes called His *Shekinah*, which literally means, "He caused to dwell" and refers to God visiting the earth with His holy, healing, powerful presence. In the gift of Jesus, God visited the earth in an unprecedented way. In the gift of the Holy Spirit, God dwells amongst us in unfathomable ways. His holy, healing, powerful presence both fills and flows through us.

Hebrews 1:3 goes on to say that "He upholds the universe by the word of His power. After making purification for sins, He sat down at the right hand of the Majesty on high." Here we see Jesus's unique contribution and calling as Creator, Redeemer and Ruler — seated at God's right hand.

This is the ultimate redemption story. Jesus, the quintessential fulfillment of God's ideal, stepped into our lives so we could step into His, inviting others to come with us as we go.

This is important, for if we have eyes to see, the world around us is filled with cries for redemption.

----

14.   Hebrews 1:2

As God's Beloved children:

We are created to Belong

We are created to Be

We are created to Contribute

And to collaborate with the Triune God to create places of deep belonging, authentic self-discovery, and meaningful contribution for others.

Lost and Found is not a kid's game. It is our life's work. Our privilege and calling in a world that so desperately needs redemption.

In the "now and not yet" way we spoke of earlier, the Gospel addresses our deepest longings. Jesus alone can be the friend who always understands, loves, and makes room for us. Through the work of the Holy Spirit alone, we can become our true selves and serve out of that Spirit-infused fullness.[15] Yet, while we await the new heaven and earth, there will always be a longing for more. A craving for deeper intimacy with God and others, a deep-seated wish that we could be more and see greater breakthroughs and progress.

We are made for and headed to a new home, a new heaven and earth, and until we get there we see merely shadows of the glory yet to come. This is the work of the church.

However, in some church traditions we have shrunk this calling, overlooking the much broader vision of "peace on earth"[16] in favor of individual salvation and personal wellbeing. As Walter Brueggemann writes, "One way the community can say 'no' to the vision and live without shalom is by deceiving itself into thinking that its private arrangements of injustice and exploitation are suitable ways of living (Jer. 6:13-14, compare Ez. 13:10,16 & Amos 6:1-6). Shalom is the special task and burden of the well-off and powerful. They are the ones held accountable for shalom."[17] How do you respond to this thought?

---

15. See, for example, Isaiah 61:1, 1 Peter 4:10.
16. Luke 2:13, 14
17. Walter Brueggemann, *Living Towards a Vision*, 24.

Prayer: "When the Divine Lover enters the human heart, all yearnings are fulfilled! Then will our mouths ring forth with laughter, and our tongues with shouts of joy: Then will we sing our songs of praise, to You, O Beloved of all hearts. For gladness will radiate out for all to see; so great is your Presence among us. Restore us to wholeness, O Healer, like newborn babes who have never strayed from you! May all who sow in tears reap with shouts of joy, leaving sorrow behind."[18]

---

18. Nan Merrill, *Psalms for Praying*, Psalm 127, 263-264.

» *Reflect on shalom for* have's *and* have-nots. *What insights do you see?*

» *What insight is offered by the juxtaposition of the worship of God and the murder of a brother in the Ghent Altarpiece?*

» *How do the trilogy of "Lost and Found" stories shape your view of restoration and redemption?*

» *The parables were given in response to a question. What was that question? What may have been beneath it? How does it make the stories even more poignant knowing they are the answer Jesus gives to this question?*

» *We have been talking about the creative tensions within and between the three pieces of this model. What additional tensions do you see in the work of restoration?*

5

God's Ideal Enacted
– in the Language and Practice of His People

TO BE GOD'S PEOPLE is to walk in His image.

To embrace and reflect the things that matter to the Trinity.

To join God in the work of *shalom*-making.

Psalm 34 reminds us to "seek peace and pursue it." The language here is active — seeking, pursuing — and could not be further from the view of "keeping the peace" through silence or compliance. As Kat Armas explains in her thought-provoking book *Abuelita Faith*: "When I began telling my experiences with racism and sexism in the church, I was quickly labelled 'divisive' . . . Speaking out against injustice isn't what divides — instead acting in ways that are divisive does. Whenever I hear the word divisive used to keep others silent from speaking up against injustice, I'm reminded of God's words spoken through Jeremiah: 'They dress the wounds of my people as though it were not serious. "Peace, peace," they say, when there is no peace' (Jer.6:14 NIV)."[1]

We have seen that *shalom* includes both right relationships and right living and are closely linked. As Mother Teresa said, "If we have no peace, it is because we have forgotten that we belong to each other."

---

1.   Kat Armas, *Abuelita Faith*, 70-71.

This shalom is antithetical to the belief that I have fulfilled the spirit of Jesus' invitation if I am personally safe and peaceful.

Martin Luther King Jr. once famously said, "No one is free until we are all free."

Audre Lorde added, "I am not free while any woman is unfree, even when her shackles are very different from my own."

Nelson Mandela once said that "to be free is not merely to cast off one's chains, but to live in such a way that respects and enhances the freedom of others."

In the same way: we do not have *shalom* until we all have it, and to have this kind of peace and wholeness means not to settle down to enjoy it but to live in such a way as to create it for others.

Peace, wholeness, and wellbeing
- with God
- within the self (physical, emotional, mental, financial, social)
- within families
- within teams and organizations
- within communities
- between people groups
- within creation
- within nations
- between nations

. . . as we can see, there is a broad scope for peacekeeping — both top-down and bottom-up.

Where does your calling best fit? And how might reframing your calling as *shalom* making/pursuing peace change the way you approach it?

On a personal level, this may involve inner healing. James 4:1 reminds us that the quarrels among us are the result of the wars within us. Peace begins here.

Where do you need the Prince of Peace to bring healing to your heart, mind and will?

On a relational level, it may involve the deep work of genuine reconciliation.

How is the health of your key relationships?

How might intentionally and wisely pursuing peace in yourself and in your relationships influence your way moving forward?

At an organizational level, peace will involve all of the above, plus the design and careful stewarding of intentionally empowering and inclusive structures and processes.

What might *shalom*-making look like in your team or organization?

We begin and end with this: as servants of the Prince of Peace, filled with the Holy Spirit of God, we called to actively pursue shalom. This includes working towards personal wholeness; and towards just, diverse, and healthy individuals, families, organizations, and communities.

May God help us as we do.

» *How is pursuing peace profoundly different from keeping the peace?*

» *How does our inner peace affect our work of peace making in the broader culture?*

» *If we were to envision the shalom work of God in our world as a puzzle what is the piece that God has uniquely created, and strategically placed you to bring?*

» *What are your most important take aways from this book?*

Conclusion

Embedded in our creation story is an invitation to God's ideal for humanity.

Belonging

Being

Contributing

Each is so deeply ingrained that to be human is to crave them.

Each is so deeply powerful that it may be a place of potential wounding for us and a place where we may hurt others.

Each is so deeply important they are a redemptive journey worth taking and a community worth co-creating.

May the Triune God guide, protect, and empower us.

And may we, the Bride of Christ enter this dance with love and faith and fervour.

"Now to Him who is able to do exceedingly abundantly above all that we ask or think, according to the power that works in us, to Him be glory in the church by Christ Jesus to all generations, forever and ever. Amen."[1]

---

1.   Ephesians 3:20-21

Bibliography

"6 Ways to Foster Belonging in the Workplace: Taking Diversity & Inclusion to the Next Level," a *Culture Amp* eBook.

Armas, Kat. *Abuelita Faith: What Women on the Margins Teach Us about Wisdom, Persistence, and Strength.* Brazos Press, 2021.

Benner, David G. *The Gift of Being Yourself.* Formatio, 2015.

Brown, Brené. *The Gifts of Imperfection.* Hazeldon, 2022.

Brueggemann, Walter. *Living Toward a Vision: Biblical Reflections on Shalom.* The Pilgrim Press, 1982.

Boers, Arthur. "What Henri Nouwen Found at Daybreak." *Christianity Today,* Oct. 3rd, 1994.

Buechner, Frederick. *Telling Secrets: a memoir.* HarperOne, 1991.

Campbell-Dollaghan, Kelsey. "A new Ikea report is an unsettling look at life in the 21st century." *Fast Company.* October 12th, 2018.

Chu, Hyon S. "New Technology Industry Diversity and Inclusion report, 2017," *Culture Amp.*

Clarkson, Adrienne. CBC Massey Lectures Series, *Belonging: The Paradox of Citizenship.* House of Anansi, 2014.

Deignan, Kathleen ed. *Thomas Merton: A Book of Hours.* Ava Maria, 2007.

Gluckstein, Dana. *Dignity: In Honor of the Rights of Indigenous Peoples.* Powerhouse Books, 2010.

Jennings, Willie. *After Whiteness: An Education in Belonging.* Eerdmans, 2020.

Job, Reuban P. *A Guide to Prayer for All God's People.* Upper Room, 1994.

Keller, Timothy. *The Meaning of Marriage: Facing the complexities of commitment with the wisdom of God.* Penguin, 2013.

Manning, Brennan. *The Relentless Tenderness of Jesus.* Baker, 2004.

Merrill, Nan. *Psalms for Praying: An Invitation to Wholeness.* Bloomsbury Academic, 2006.

Merton, Thomas. *New Seeds of Contemplation.* New Directions, 1987.

Merton, Thomas. *Thoughts in Solitude.* Shambhala, 1956.

Moore, Beth. *Breaking Free: The Journey, The Stories.* Lifeway, 2009.

Nouwen, Henri. *In the Name of Jesus: Reflections on Christian Leadership.* Crossroad, 1992.

Nouwen, Henri. *Life of the Beloved.* Crossroads, 1992.

Nouwen, Henri. *The Return of the Prodigal Son: A Story of Homecoming.* Doubleday, 1994.

Palmer, Parker. *Let Your Life Speak: Listening for the Voice of Vocation.* Jossey-Bass, 2000.

Purifoy, Christie. *Roots and Wings: A Journey Home in Four Seasons.* Baker, 2016.

Reyes, Patrick. *Nobody Cries When We Die: God, Community and Surviving to Adulthood.* Nashville: Chalice, 2016. ProQuest eBook Central.

Richardson, Jan. *In the Sanctuary of Women: A Companion for Reflection and Prayer.* Upper Room, 2010.

Rimer, Sara. "For Girls, It's Be Yourself, and Be Perfect, Too," *NY Times*, April 1, 2007.

Root, Andrew. *Revisiting Relational Ministry: From a Strategy of Influence to a Theology of Incarnation.* IVP Books, 2007.

Scazzero, Peter. *Emotionally Healthy Spirituality.* Thomas Nelson, 2006.

Sweet, Leonard and Frank Viola. *Jesus: A Theography.* Thomas Nelson, 2012.

Turnbull, Colin. *The Mountain People.* Touchstone, 1987.

Tutu, Desmond. *No Future Without Forgiveness.* Doubleday, 1999.

Volf, Miroslav. *Exclusion and Embrace: A Theological Exploration of Identity, Otherness, and Reconciliation.* Abingdon, 1996.

Wheatley, Margaret and Deborah Frieze. *Walk Out Walk On: A Learning Journey Into Communities Daring to Live the Future Now.* BK Publishers, 2011.